WINTER
ADVENTURE

A COMPLETE GUIDE
TO WINTER SPORTS
BY
PETER STARK AND
STEVEN M. KRAUZER

A TRAILSIDE SERIES GUIDE

W. W. NORTON & COMPANY

NEW YORK   LONDON

Look for these other Trailside® Series Guides:

Bicycling: Touring and Mountain Bike Basics
Cross-Country Skiing: A Complete Guide
Hiking & Backpacking: A Complete Guide
Kayaking: Whitewater and Touring Basics

Trailside is a registered trademark of New Media, Inc.

First Edition

The text of this book is composed in Bodoni Book with the display set in Triplex
Page composition by Tina Christensen Design
Color separations and prepress by Bergman Graphics, Incorporated
Manufacturing by R. R. Donnelley & Sons
Illustrations by Ron Hildebrand

Book design by Bill Harvey

Library of Congress Cataloging-in-Publication Data

Stark, Peter, 1954–
Winter Adventure: a complete guide/by Peter Stark and Steven M. Krauzer;
    p. cm. – (A Trailside series guide)
    Includes bibliographical references and index.
    1. Winter Sports. I. Krauzer, Steven M. II. Title. III. Series.
    GV841.S83   1995   796.9:–dc20   95-34646

ISBN 0-393-31400-6

W. W. Norton & Company, Inc., 500 Fifth Avenue, New York, NY 10110
W. W. Norton & Company Ltd., 10 Coptic Street, London WC1A 1PU

1 2 3 4 5 6 7 8 9 0

C O N T E N T S

PREFACE

Our purpose in *Winter Adventure: A Complete Guide to Winter Sports* is to suggest new horizons in the cold season, in the form of over two dozen sports, activities, and games, as well as ways to explore the winter wilderness.

You may have tried some of these adventures as a child; others will be new to you. Our aim is to remind you that all of them are out there for the trying, and generally accessible and reasonably easy to learn for anyone who possesses the spirit of exploration and fun.

USING THIS BOOK

Winter Adventure is somewhat different from other volumes in the Trailside series in that it is not necessarily comprehensive in its instruction. Rather its purpose is to introduce you to an activity, tell you what to expect, and provide enough information to get you started.

These pursuits vary in the expertise and experience each demands. The chapter on sledding, for example, will more than adequately prepare you to hit the slopes — and, we hope, leave you eager to do so. With the chapters on snowboarding and ice climbing, however, you'll likely want to seek out instruction from an expert, as we did. The Sources & Resources section will point you in the direction of further information.

While few of these sports are expensive in terms of equipment — and many will cost you virtually nothing — some of the gear borders on the esoteric. A list of mail-order suppliers of such gear appears in Sources & Resources.

We've chosen to focus on sports that require individual initiative over massive investment in equipment and trips to expensive resorts. Thus downhill skiing is not represented (there are plenty of excellent instructional books available), while cross-country skiing has its own Trailside volume.

WHO "WE" ARE

The many anecdotes in this book that relate our experiences are meant to give a feeling of "hands-on" participation. In relating them, the two authors have chosen to refer to themselves with the pronoun "we" except where the personal nature of the anecdote made doing so seem especially awkward.

In fact, the authors have been close friends for years and have spent many days pursuing adventures together in the winter outdoors. However, you'll understand that in some of the episodes described here only one of us was there in person.

But in every case, we were both present in spirit. The two of us share the winter passion, and our goal is to instill that same passion in you.

INTRODUCTION

Last winter we happened to be in Manhattan when snowfall visited the city. We thought it delightful to walk through the urban canyons and watch the snowflakes dancing down between the skyscrapers, blanketing the parks, frosting the trees. But when we returned to a friend's apartment and turned on the evening news, we wondered if we'd missed something.

It sounded as if New York City were under siege.

The reporters and weatherpeople described the snowstorm in terms of warfare. A "winter assault" gripped the city in its "dangerous hold." The inhabitants had suffered a "brutal month" of "miserable conditions." One correspondent glared up at the gray sky, noted a few flurries drifting gently down, and hissed into the microphone that they were "taunting" him.

It's not just New York City; all over snow country winter is often described as a hostile, deadly force. It's no wonder that so many Americans try to run or hide from it. They flee to the warm oceans and balmy breezes of the South or hunker down indoors, wrapped in blankets and huddled in front of space heaters, shuddering at reports of slick streets, plummeting temperatures, and howling winds. The underlying message of this anti-winter propaganda is that, to paraphrase Noel Coward, only mad dogs and Englishmen would go out in weather like this.

In fact, we wonder (tongue in cheek) if the first English colonists, rather than present-day media prophets of winter doom, are to blame for Americans' lousy attitude toward winter. The British had good reason to dislike the darker months — the United Kingdom is notorious for its soggy, rainy, chilly winters. Without snow or ice or real cold

> ❝ The wonder of a single snowflake outweighs the wisdom of a million meteorologists. ❞
>
> — Sir Francis Bacon

except in the Scottish high country, the typical English winter offers little in the way of amusing outdoor activities other than the opportunity to sit before a glowing peat fire with a hot drink.

This misconceived notion of winter has remained in many Americans' psyches through the generations, but it does not match the reality of winter on this continent. In much of the United States, winters are not dank but crisp; it is a season where nature freezes solid. Winter glistens with snowy beauty and frozen grace, offering endless possibilities for outdoor activities that are wildly unlike anything you can find in the summer months.

We wonder if Americans might feel differently about winter if the Norwegians had been the first to land at Plymouth Rock.

Scandinavians *love* winter and excel at inventing ways to amuse themselves in the snow. These are people whose national sport is cross-country skiing; in these countries, tens of thousands of city dwellers can be seen gliding across snowy parks and frozen ponds on a winter's Sunday afternoon, and, quite unlike New York City, people grow depressed and angry if it doesn't snow. In short, Scandinavians know how to embrace winter rather than run and hide from it.

We argue that you too should learn to love winter, to revel in it and celebrate it. To do so, you have to be active in it, whether you're sledding, skating, snowshoeing, animal tracking, or indulging in any of the many other activities treated in these pages. We promise that you'll be warmer and happier embracing winter, rather than hiding from it in a drafty living room staring morosely at the storm outside your picture window.

Yes, we've heard the usual objections. They go like this:

I'm a warm-blooded person.

Ice and snow are too slippery and I can't get around.

I'd like to get outdoors but winter sports are too strenuous/too difficult to learn.

All those skis and skates and

other equipment are too expensive and so much hassle.

Let's deflate these objections in order.

As we enjoyed the Manhattan snowstorm, we watched businessmen hurrying down the street hugging themselves against the cold wind, bare-headed, gloveless, and shod in thin leather shoes. No wonder they were so miserable. For starters, you lose more than a tenth of your body heat through your head. That "warm-blooded person" who can't stand the cold is actually a person who doesn't dress properly (see Chapter 14).

As for the slipperiness of snow and ice, that's a great part of winter's charm, and the trick is to use that slipperiness to have fun. We think of winter's slippery surfaces as *liberating* us from the plodding friction of hot asphalt or gritty concrete. For example, ice — one of the most slippery substances nature produces — allows you to glide and spin and swoop in long, effortless strokes faster, more easily, and more gracefully than you could ever run on dry land.

Take skating. Instead of freedom of movement, too many people acquaint it with jostling crowds on a tiny rectangle of artificial ice in the atrium of a shopping mall. For us, skating is the beauty of coursing freely over the polished surface of a pond or lake, exploring its shores, gazing through its crystalline surface at the still life of rocks and weeds on the bottom. You experience not only a different type of movement but a whole new world.

Winter sports are much easier to learn than most people imagine. All of the activities described in this book can be enjoyed by anyone in reasonable physical shape who goes at them with an enthusiastic attitude. Most can be attempted by your own experimentation and initiative, a few through lessons or by engaging a guide. To become an *expert*, of course, demands a lot of hard work, but that applies to any sport, winter or summer.

But, also as in any other sport, there is no need or pressure to seek the heights, and it's likely you'll gain a greater satisfaction from your earliest, "I think I've got it," efforts than from aspirations to be flawless. The level to which you wish to rise is up to you, but in every case, the entry level is eminently pleasurable. A high-level skater remembers her first triple axel, but we'll bet that the skater recalls with more vividness the time she was able to stand up on skates, put off across the pond, and not fall down.

In some of these activities, the gap between absolute beginner and proficiency is not that wide. With snowshoeing, for example, the standard joke goes, "What separates a novice from an expert?" The answer: "Six steps."

Snowshoeing is, like many of the sports in this book, surprisingly inexpensive. The pricey image of winter sports likely stems from the downhill skiing industry, which has never shied from promoting its upscale glamour. As you'll see, many of the sports we enjoy are, save for a minimal investment in equipment, virtually free.

Your investment in winter pays a spiritual dividend as well. Have you ever noticed how much nicer people are to each other during a snowstorm? Or when they encounter each other in a snowy woods? We warily keep each other at arm's length in summer's heat, but winter draws us nearer to other humans. We like to think of winter as a warming of the human spirit.

We are the proselytizers of winter. We tell people over and over: "Why run and hide from a season that amounts to one-quarter of your life?" We have a friend who moved from a large eastern city to Montana, and packed his lousy attitude about winter in his baggage. That first year he spent from November to March huddled in his drafty house, grumpily flicking between basketball games and soaps.

WINTER TALES

The notion of winter as a time of barrenness, desolation, depression, and even death is unfortunately reinforced throughout our literary tradition. In the very first line that William Shakespeare penned for Richard the Third, the king bemoans "the winter of our discontent." For the Bard, the season is "Barren winter, with his wrathful nipping cold," and he suggests that "A sad tale's best for winter."

Shakespeare's contemporaries were no more enamored of our favorite season. Poet George Herbert complains that "Every mile is two in winter," while essayist Thomas Nashe pleads, "From winter, plague and pestilence, good Lord, deliver us!"

At about the same time, on the other side of the Atlantic, Governor William Bradford described the attitude toward winter of the Pilgrims of Plymouth Plantation:

> And for the season it was winter, and they that know the winters of that country know them to be sharp and violent, and subject to cruel and fierce storms, dangerous to travel to known places, much more to search an unknown coast. . . . For summer being done, all things stand upon them with a weather-beaten

continued on next page

face, and the whole country, full of woods and thickets, represented a wild and savage hue.

A recurring literary metaphor styles winter in good-news/bad-news
terms, with the good news being that the darned season can't last forever. "Rise up, my love, my fair one, and come away," King Solomon
writes in the Old Testament. "For, lo, the winter is past, the rain is over
and gone." Governor Bradford's fellow colonist, the early American poet
Anne Bradstreet, characterizes the early months as an uplifting moral
lesson, noting that "If we had not winter, the spring would not be so
pleasant; if we did not sometimes taste of adversity, prosperity would not
be so welcome."

We of course prefer those literateurs who view winter more benignly
— or at least with tongue in cheek. Lord Byron, for example, refers with
stolid resignation to "The English winter — ending in July, To recom-
mence in August," and Stanislaw Jerzy Lec points out that "No
snowflake in an avalanche ever feels responsible."

The second winter we introduced
him to backcountry skiing. He began
to go out on his own, first once a week,
then twice a week, then three times a
week. He kept lists of the animal
tracks he identified in the snow. "It's
so peaceful in the woods in winter," he
told us. "It's another world."

The third winter we showed him
the sled run we'd built on a mountainside near town. In the beginning
he was skeptical — "How do you
stop the thing?" — but after that first
wild, snow-spraying ride, he climbed
back up the mountain eager for
another run. Now he's learning to ice-
skate. His biggest obstacle is figuring
out how to fit all the winter activities
into his schedule. "I'm outdoors more
in the winter than I am in the
summer," he says. Meanwhile, his
television remote control gathers
dust.

What follows is a step-by-step
guide to teach *you* how to love winter,
too.

SLEDDING

Ⓞne winter several years ago, a magazine dispatched us to the Winter Olympic complex at Lake Placid. Our assignment: Learn to ride a luge.

We had not sledded since childhood. We considered it a chaotic, simple, kids-only pursuit and, in our adulthood, we preferred more challenging winter sports. But that single week in upstate New York totally changed our thinking. Reclining on small, graceful, responsive sleds while rocketing down a twisting tube of glassy ice recalled to us the adventure and sheer fun of sledding, and provided all the challenge we could ask for.

When we returned home to Montana, we immediately went to work constructing our own "luge" run on the steep ridgeline of Mount Jumbo, which rises a thousand feet above our backyard. Over time we extended the run higher and packed it harder, until we'd created our masterpiece: a sled track nearly a mile long and dropping 1,000 vertical feet, through screaming straightways, hairpin curves, and the sharp, stomach-flipping drop-offs known in British sledding lingo as "leaps."

The true beauty of our run was that a sledder of *any* ability could enjoy it. Young or more tentative sledders spun and shrieked on

important, encourages that carefree abandon to the world of snow and ice that, in our mind, epitomizes winter sport.

While ancient sled designs remain in the form of toboggans and Scandinavian *pulkas*, perhaps 90 percent of American children now slide downhill on molded plastic.

SLEDDING HISTORY

The sled is one of man's earliest vehicles and probably was first used to haul game by hunters. It then developed into its many permutations in northern regions around the globe — the dogsled of the Eskimos, the toboggan of the North American Indians, and the *pulka* of the Laplanders, which looks like a sawed-off canoe towed by reindeer.

saucers or plastic toboggans as they negotiated its gentle lower slopes. The more adventurous pushed off from the head of the steep chute at the very top for a snow-spraying, white-knuckle ride that demanded cool nerves and split-second timing to avoid launching out of a curve and flying face-first into a snowbank.

Here is the essence of sledding: It spans a spectrum from the most basic act of sliding down a slippery slope to, at the upper levels of competition, a sophisticated sport in which professional athletes roar through multimillion-dollar half-pipes of ice on precision Italian-built racing bobs.

Besides offering something for any age, athletic ability, or ambition, sledding provides exercise (a Stairmaster, after all, mimics the action of climbing a sledding hill); is inexpensive and requires little gear; and, most

Children soon discovered that they could slide wildly down snowy hills on sleds constructed of wood and bone. On this continent, Native American children were fond of sledding, as were the European children who arrived with the colonists. By the time of the American Revolution, Boston Common was home to the most famous sledding hill in the New World. During the British occupation in the winter of 1775-76, that slope found its way into the history books.

Troops billeted nearby (on about the present site of the Massachusetts

State House) had made a hash of the hill with comings and goings, according to an account in *Boston Common: A Diary of Notable Events, Incidents and Neighboring Occurences*, published by Samuel Butler in 1914. Fed up, the children marched to General Thomas Gage with their grievance.

"What!" he demanded, "have your fathers been teaching you rebellion, and sent you here to exhibit it?"

"Nobody sent us, sir," one boy replied, "but yesterday our slides were destroyed once more; and we will bear it no longer!"

Gage, impressed with their "love of liberty in the air they breathed," gave his guarantee that the children's hallowed hill would henceforth be unmolested.

While recreational tobogganing enjoyed popularity

among adults in this country during the late 1800s, at about the same time the British upper classes were elevating sledding to a competitive sport. Wintering in the spas of the Swiss Alps, they seized upon the small sleds known as *handschlitten*, ridden by schoolchildren for sport and used by postmen and farmers to haul small loads. Piloting these sitting upright, the British challenged each other to races down the twisting mountain roads.

Friendly rivalries soon

developed between teams representing neighboring resorts, leading to formal dashes on longer and more elaborately designed courses. Eventually this evolved into the sports of luge and skeleton riding. In the former, participants lie on their back on a high-tech version of the *handschlitten*, while in skeleton, or Cresta, riding they lie on their stomachs and descend headfirst.

The earliest sleds on both sides of the Atlantic shared one feature: None had a steering device. You changed course by shifting weight, dragging a hand or foot, or jumping the runners to either side. This changed when Samuel Allen, a Philadelphia manufacturer of farm implements, invented the steerable sled. In Allen's ingenious design, pulling a handlebar bent the front of the flexible steel runners

DID YOU KNOW

The first and perhaps most famous sledding run is the Cresta, at St. Moritz, Switzerland. Built under the supervision of Major W. H. Bulpett in 1884, the 1,327-yard track remains in use today. Riders routinely hit speeds of 80 miles an hour as they rocket through huge banked curves with names like "Battledore" and "Shuttlecock."

and veered the sled in the direction the sledder wished to travel.

Allen's sled went on the market in 1889, at a retail price of between $2.25 and $5 depending on length. It was an immediate best-seller. Rigid-railed sleds were a thing of the past; Allen's Flexible Flyer did for sledding what the Wright Brothers would soon do for flight. Substantially unchanged in design, the Flyer remains a popular sled a century later.

CHOOSING A SLED

Sleds today come in dozens of varieties, each with its distinct personality and style of riding. Your choice, like finding a mate, is strictly a matter of personal preference. Much depends on how seriously you wish to pursue the sport. Here are the four broad categories of sleds, in roughly ascending order of sophistication:

Makeshift sleds include — but are by no means limited to — inner tubes, plastic garbage bags, air mattresses, shovels (you can actually find organized shovel races in Wisconsin), and that proverbial favorite among college students, the cafeteria tray. Besides their lack of expense, the most notable quality of these sleds is that they also lack any means of control. You're treated to a wild, spinning ride, sometimes forward, sometimes backward, and often upside down in a snowbank — which is precisely the point for a certain breed of happy-go-lucky, throw-fate-to-the-wind sledders.

Mold-injected plastic sleds in the shape of disks, saucers, wedges, and toboggan-like troughs, in common with the makeshift category of sleds, usually lack steering mechanisms. On most, you may sit upright or lie prone. No turns here; these whisk you straight down the hill as you flail and fly over bumps. From our observations at sled hills around the country, we'd guess that about 90 percent of sledding in the United States is of this variety.

The beautifully crafted *wooden toboggan* has changed little since its invention by pre-Columbian Native Americans.

It is built of long strips of wood steam-bent into a graceful curve at the front and fastened with wooden cross-struts, and the deck may be equipped with a pad. The advantage of a toboggan is that the whole family can pile on and ride it downhill. It can be steered in a rudimentary fashion by the

1) The flying saucer, least controllable of all sleds; 2) the classic Flexible Flyer, most controllable of widely available sleds; and 3) the toboggan, descendent of the pre-Columbian Native American craft.

Start of the "tourist" luge at Lake Placid, New York, where anyone can experience the thrill of high-speed banked curves on an iced track.

person in front, through twisting the upturned prow. It is usually ridden in a seated position, with the legs of each person under the arms of the person in front. Less commonly, riders kneel, but this has its pitfalls; as a kid, I chipped a tooth when, on hitting a bump, the boy in front kicked me in the face.

Samuel Allen's *Flexible Flyer–type sled*, the classic kids' holiday gift, represents a major step up in sophistication, but is still a sled that any eight-year-old child can learn to use in a trice. Although you can ride a Flyer in a sitting position while manipulating the steering bar with your feet, the preferred technique is "belly-whomping," diving face-down onto the deck as you launch, and

HIGH-PERFORMANCE SLEDS

After our return from Lake Placid, we became interested in the less-well-known types of sleds. We discovered a whole class not widely available in the United States, which we might call naturbahn or luge sleds. These are steerable sleds that you ride sitting feet-first or lying on your back.

Two of our discoveries are of particular note. From a manufacturer in Germany we obtained what is inarguably the most elegant

recreational snow-runner we've used. It has plastic-and-wood-laminate ski-type runners, a small hardwood deck, and two heavy-gauge plastic handles beside the rider's hips. You ride sitting up, and steer by pulling on one handle and pressing down on the opposite ski tip so the entire sled flexes.

We found that this high-performance sled demanded a good bit of skill to keep upright through a turn, but it was handled with aplomb by our teenaged friend Cameron Porter, whose surfing experience in his hometown of

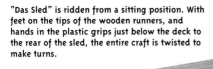

"Das Sled" is ridden from a sitting position. With feet on the tips of the wooden runners, and hands in the plastic grips just below the deck to the rear of the sled, the entire craft is twisted to make turns.

working the steering bar by hand.

A Flyer allows you to make turns or maneuver through impromptu slalom courses, but what you gain in performance you lose in versatility. With its slender steel runners, it glides much faster than the plastic sliding devices if the snow is firmly packed on the sledding hill, but, unlike the plastic devices, tends to bog down in soft snow. Flyers come in varying lengths; the longest, at 60 inches, will accommodate the average adult.

Sydney, Australia, made him feel right at home on what we'd dubbed "Das Sled."

We also got our hands on a naturbahn luge. This consists of arched wooden runners that support a canvas sling instead of the usual wooden deck. Sitting or semi-supine, the sledder steers by pressing a foot against one of the upturned runners, or by dragging a hand behind.

Naturbahn has been a popular European sport for some time, but is only now beginning to catch on in the States. As the name sug-gests, this is luging on a "natural road," a course designed to use existing features of the hill that may be enhanced by the banking of snow. This course can be set up on virtually any sledding hill or ski slope, requiring only packed snow rather than the laboriously created ice of formal luge tracks. In com-petition, naturbahn riders compete against the clock; in the United States, there's a course near Mar-quette, Michigan (see Sources and Resources for details).

that in itself makes the search for the perfect hill rewarding. Fine sledding hills are not difficult to discover, if you know what to look for.

Choosing a Hill

You want an open slope roughly between 10 and 20 degrees (a 20-degree hill rises 20 feet for every 90 linear feet). It should be free of trees, large rocks, and

The ideal sledding hill is steep, broad, clear of obstructions, and has a long, clear run-out. A send-off from your grandmother is icing on the cake!

SLOPES AND SNOW CONDITIONS

One of my most vivid boyhood memories is sledding at night down my parents' steep, twisting driveway. As the steel runners of my Flexible Flyer skim over the glazed, tire-packed snow, they strike embedded bits of gravel and toss off contrails of brilliant sparks. I feel as if I am riding a rocket that blazes across that dark winter sky.

Hills like this — and the moments of sledding they provide — become etched in your mind, and

structures, and end in a wide, long, flat runout unobstructed by road or fence (see "Sledding Safety," page 24). Hilly golf-course fairways have long been favorite sledding hills. The broad lawns of city parks also often offer a hill long and steep enough for a good ride. Once you have your "sled legs," consider heading into the backcountry (see page 26, "Ever Higher Up the Hill").

Fine-Tuning Your Course

If the snow lies deep and soft, you may have to pack it, depending on your model of sled. The broad bottom of a toboggan or plastic saucer works on both softer deeper snow and a packed surface, but a Flyer's narrow rails require some snow grooming.

For those fortunate enough to have willing parents, a sled can serve as transportation to and from a favorite hill.

The easiest way to pack is simply to start with several runs on a flat-bottomed sled so your traffic compacts the snow. You can also step up or down the hill on a pair of skis to pack it out. One trick we've used is to duct-tape a bundle of firewood to a small toboggan and drag it up the run as we climb. Not only does it groom the run, but it provides a vehicle for riding back down.

SLEDDING TECHNIQUE

Some sleds don't require any technique whatsoever. You simply get on, hold tightly, and let the sled whisk you away downhill. This type of sledding appeals especially to smaller children. Watch the way they delightedly abandon themselves and shout out their pleasure at the twists and turns of a saucer ride.

But with more sledding experience, you or your children will probably get a hankering to steer the sled in the direction you wish to go. Eventually, you may set up a course and start racing each other; in this case, you'll need to refine your steering technique. It will differ among sled types, but a few general principles apply.

Prone or sitting on "unsteerable" devices like a cafeteria tray or plastic toboggan, you can change direction in a crude fashion by dragging your feet or hands. To turn right, drag a right foot or right hand; vice versa for left. You apply the brakes by dragging both feet. The one exception to this is the saucer, which is designed to be totally unsteerable to give the wildest, most unpredictable ride.

A Flyer, in contrast, is eminently steerable, though the technique has a surprising variety of refinements. For a simple turn on packed snow, you merely crank the bar to flex the run-

The best sledding hills are easily identified: Within hours of a fresh snowfall they are "seasoned" by countless sled trails, which pack the snow and make the runs even faster.

ners, but you'll need more "body English" in specialized turning situations. We learned this lesson when, while attempting to veer sharply, we outdid our own strength and ripped the bar clean off the sled.

To augment your turn, dig in with the toe of the boot on the turning side. It helps to keep your weight back; a Flyer's sensitive — and somewhat delicate — rails require little down-pressure to "bite." I totaled another sled by ignoring this advice; as I missed a curve and hit deep snow, my weight, combined with the flexion on the runner, collapsed it into the bottom of the deck.

SLEDDING SAFETY

A surprising number of sprains, contusions, broken bones, and other injuries — including fatalities — result from what appears to be the most innocent of winter sports. Many a beginning sledder simply doesn't understand how badly he can hurt himself when his speeding body collides with a stationary object such as a tree or a fence. Before allowing the excitement of the moment to overtake you when you're about to push off from the summit, consider some elementary precautions.

Standard winter garb with all its

layers (see Chapter 14, "Dressing for Winter") lends itself to sledding through its inherent cushioning. If you plan to toe-drag for braking and steering, you'll want boots with sturdy toes and soles that won't delaminate. Wear a helmet and goggles if you attempt higher speeds or trickier courses. For further padding, consider "dressing" your sled as well. Ever since I suffered saucer-sized bruises on the thighs from hitting the rails of my Flyer during jumps, I've retrofitted the decks with 3-inch foam rubber (available at a fabric shop).

gentle leap when you started halfway up the hill may flatten you with the impact of landing if you take it from the top. If you are sitting on a sled or toboggan when it takes to the air, it's prudent to lean forward or back rather than sitting straight up, in order to help your spine flex and absorb the impact of landing.

Well-bundled sledders lined-up for another run. Hats, gloves, and scarves are all recommended. Felt-lined rubber boots are a must if small toes are to remain warm.

Hitting an obstacle is the most common cause of sledding mishap. Always choose an open slope with a sufficiently long and flat runout at the bottom.

If you sled on a snowpacked driveway or road, post a person at the top and bottom to stop oncoming traffic until sledders have passed.

While bumps and jumps are part of the sledding experience, use common sense in determining how far you want to fly. What was a

Don't underestimate your potential for speed. With the right sled, the right snow, and the right hill, you can glide faster than you believed possible; riders belly-whomping down the Cresta run reach speeds of 80 miles per hour. Work your way up the hill a bit at a time to get a feeling for its potential for velocity.

Don't pile people one on top of the other on a sled or toboggan, at the risk of seriously body-slamming the lower party. We know of a fatality

The favored Flexible Flyer position. It is not for the faint of heart.

quently. Most likely you'll skid to a stop. Try to keep a hand on the sled so it doesn't run away downhill without you — and always remember you have the option of "bailing out" if you're going faster than you wish, by simply dumping over onto the forgiving surface.

EVER HIGHER UP THE HILL

After a while, a straight run down the local sledding hill may not bring the same thrill it did at first. In that case, it is time to seek new, more exciting horizons.

that occurred when eight men piled on a giant sled and rode it over a jump, the combined weight of the top seven crushing the bottom rider.

Simply falling off a moving sled is rarely a risk and occurs fre-

The sled run we built far up the flanks of Mount Jumbo was in effect a naturbahn course, with its twists and turns and drops. We measured it with a 100-foot length of plastic rope, then wrote a computer program that converted our digital-watch-measured times over various sections into speed. The record is 30.1354 miles per hour, achieved on glare ice with a running start down on a 35-degree section we call Dead Man's Leap.

Still, our version of naturbahn began to feel tame, so we've taken sledding a step further to what, tongue partly in cheek, we call "expeditionary luging." We wait for the mountain snowpack to firm up, then set out on a sunny spring morning to hike up some nearby peak with our sleds lashed to our backs. After a picnic lunch on top of the bald summit, we launch into a wild "first descent" down a snowy cirque.

The ultimate sledding experience, however, is to ride a luge, bobsled, or skeleton through the high-speed banked curves of an iced track. During our trip to Lake Placid, we were surprised that the luge authorities not only allowed members of the general public to luge, but encouraged it.

You pay fees to join the U.S. Luge Association and a local luge club, and are provided with the necessary equipment and a coach. You can also take a single ride on a luge from halfway up the track for $15, or climb aboard as a passenger on a bobsled on a pay-per-ride basis. (At the moment, the Lake Placid track is the only full-scale luge track in the United States, but one exists at Calgary, Alberta, and one is under con-

struction at Salt Lake City, Utah.)

That first morning, we joined a small coterie of beginners who were suited up in sweatsuits, helmets, and running shoes, and climbed partway up the snowy path beside the track. We listened closely — very closely — as Dmitry, a young Russian émigré luge expert and former dog groomer, instructed us in the use of the sled.

The track dispatcher, who sat above the run in what looked like an airport control tower, periodically called another "sled on the track." We'd hear a low rumbling sound and suddenly a black streak would shoot by with an explosive whir and flash.

These were the members of the national team taking their morning practice runs. Each wore a rubberized suit that made the "slider" look like a space alien, and lay flat on his or her back on a sled that resembled a miniature La-Z Boy recliner mounted on a pair of diamond-polished steel runners. One of the sliders momentarily lost control high up on the big wall of Curve 10. The sled runners emitted a horrendous shriek that sounded like a giant set of fingernails on a blackboard, as the rider tried to keep from ramming into the wooden barrier across the curve's top.

Our little group fell silent. We were all thinking the same thing. "How do we avoid the big crash?" someone finally asked.

Dmitry reassured us that we would be going slowly at first. One by one he sent the beginners down the lower portion of the track. When it was my turn, Dmitry jokingly made the sign of the cross over me and gave me a little shove. Those first runs were slow and easy — it felt like I was trundling downhill on a chaise longue through a world of white. But each day, as I moved higher up the track, my reclining chair gathered a little more speed.

We were finally ready to attempt a run from the "ladies' start." What worried us was the spot about two-thirds of the way down that sliders had dubbed "the Hogpen." This was a short section between two difficult turns: If you weren't perfectly set up as you left the first, you ricocheted off the walls and came off your sled in the second. I'd already nearly lost it in the Hogpen once before, my sled skidding and screeching wildly, careening like a pinball off the ice walls before it somehow straightened out.

"In the beginning, it's fun," Dmitry said philosophically after our scare. "Then you go higher up the track and it's not so much fun — you fall off the sled and take bad beatings. But then you start cooking and it's the biggest fun. It's like you go in Audi 4000" — he grabbed an imaginary steering wheel and stomped on its accelerator with his pac boots — "zzzooommm!"

Yes indeed, that's how it felt on that final run from the ladies' start. I shot out of a long straightaway toward the big wall of Curve 10 and the world of white flipped to the left. The *g* forces plastered me to the sled and the sled to the wall, tugging my head and limbs toward the white ice. Suddenly the world flipped back the other way into the long horseshoe of Turn 11 and I was riding it, riding it, into quick Turn 12.

And there it was: the Hogpen. I knew I had to stay relaxed to keep a stable sled. I couldn't turn too early. I delayed a moment, then steered hard with shoulder and foot, just now, and suddenly I was through it, hitting the right line like threading a needle.

The sound of the runners no longer reminded me of a scream. In fact, they seemed to whir cheerily as I headed on down toward the end of the track.

S N O W S H O E I N G

I n the popular mind, snowshoeing is associated with French Canadian explorers in the deep North Woods, grizzled mountain men tending trap lines in the High Rockies, and gold-crazed prospectors in the unforgiving Klondike. The fact of the matter is that snowshoeing is probably the most accessible and easiest to learn of all winter sports. If you can walk, you can snowshoe.

That's one of the reasons snowshoeing is currently undergoing a renaissance. But another, more important factor is that snowshoes offer the perfect means for exploring nature in winter, whether you want to track animals, wend through the frosted forest to look and listen, or simply beat that case of cabin fever with a little vigorous exercise.

Until a recent trip to Aspen, Colorado, I hadn't snowshoed for 30 years, when as a youth I strapped on my grandfather's big old Yukon models and tromped around the backyard during a Wisconsin blizzard. I'd traveled to Aspen because I'd heard the winter resort had become one center of an explosion of interest in snowshoeing, but I was unprepared for its extent. I found snowshoe races, snowshoe nature tours through the backcountry, and even a snowshoe manufacturing plant.

Snowshoes, like so much of our modern sporting equipment, have become high-tech. Crafted from nylon and aluminum, the modern designs are much smaller and easier to handle than Grandfather's great webbed feet. Snowshoeing has changed as well, at least for some. In the hyper-athletic town of Aspen, I saw people in purple Lycra tights racing each other up the packed slopes of ski runs at sprint speed, on tiny lightweight snowshoes that looked almost like no snowshoes at all.

This struck me as quizzical. I was after the experience where snowshoes had a purpose — the purpose they've always had, of providing a means of floating atop deep powder instead of having one's legs sinking into it to the thighs, like two fence posts in quick-

sand. I asked around, and presently found myself at the pottery studio of Molly Heizer.

Molly, a former snowshoe guide, and her boyfriend, John Dufficy, a climbing and ski guide, are back-country snowshoe enthusiasts and experts, and the backcountry happens to be right outside Molly's door. She handed me a pair of light-weight snowshoes called Sherpas. As I bent to lash them to my feet, her three Labrador retrievers nuzzled me energeti-cally, sensing an expedition in the offing.

THE LEARNING CURVE

To don the Sherpas, we simply slipped our hiking boots into a pocket of fabric and tied them in with nylon bindings that ran through hooks like a shoelace. We tightened heel straps and that was it — we were ready to roll.

We looped into ski poles (most snowshoers these days use poles to aid

Snowshoes — with their unbeatable stability and traction — can be ideal for winter pack trips, as here, near Wyoming's Grand Tetons.

their balance), crossed the muddy driveway, and clambered up a steep snowbank. A snowshoe binding, like that of a cross-country ski, allows you to lift your heel. Beneath it on the underside of the snowshoe is a serrated metal footplate, or cleat, that grips the snow for steep or icy climbs. The shoes easily held their traction as we ascended the bank.

John, Molly, and I proceeded up a broad, snowy mountainside into an

GEAR TALK

BOUND FEET AND FROZEN FINGERS

The weak link that has long frustrated beginning snowshoers is the binding that attaches one's boot to the snowshoe. Early snowshoes used a system of straps that often worked loose while tramping through deep snow or slipped off the heel while walking downhill, requiring the snowshoer to dig into the snow with naked fingers to retighten the bindings. Today's snowshoe manufacturers such as Tubbs have devised a stiff, molded plastic binding that fits a boot — any winter boot will do — and is hinged to the frame. Your feet stay in your bindings and your fingers stay in your mittens.

When descending very steep slopes, turn to face uphill and sidestep across the slope. The same maneuver can be used when ascending.

aspen forest, Molly in her red jump-suit breaking trail ahead, the dogs looping around us. "Is there any special technique we should know about?" I asked.

"No," she called back. "Just walk."

And that was it. In those first steps I'd gone from novice to — well, if not expert, at least a competent snowshoer.

The wet, crusty snow on this spring day lay probably 3 or 4 feet deep; in hiking boots alone, travel would have been like trying to traverse a wading pond filled with freshly poured cement. The exertion of wading through deep snow is huge,

SNOWSHOE HISTORY

The earliest known snowshoes are solid wood, essentially planks strapped to the feet, and place the first snowshoers in Central and Northern Asia, and in Scandinavia. Bogs in the latter have yielded examples of these ski/snowshoe hybrids that are between 4,000 and 5,000 years old.

Historians believe the snow-shoe crossed from Asia to North America during the early human migrations over the Bering Land Bridge. Snowshoeing expert Gene Prater believes that the Native Americans studied the feet of snow-going animals as inspiration for designs of snowshoes. Beavertail snowshoes resemble the hind feet of the snowshoe hare, he writes.

However it arrived and evolved, snowshoe-making rose to an art form among the native peoples of North America. With its steamed-wood frame and intricate webbing, the snowshoe evolved in many variations of size and shape to address the great variety of powdery snow conditions in North America's forests, while the Scandinavians developed the fast, narrow ski to take advantage of the firmer snow found in their more open terrain.

Modern snowshoes are relatively narrow, and so don't require the wide, awkward stance of earlier designs. Combined with light weight, these snowshoes allow for almost graceful sprinting.

which is why prehistoric hunter-gatherers invented the snowshoe. If they had to extract a foot after each step, the trek would cost more energy than the food obtained could replace.

With older-style snowshoes, you had to walk with your feet wide apart to prevent stepping on one shoe with the other. Modern snowshoes are narrower and don't require this broad stance, although some people find they have to spread their feet slightly. Molly said that in her experience people rarely trip over their shoes unless they change models and have to accustom themselves to a modified stance.

The creamy bare trunks of the aspen trees marching endlessly up the slope reminded us of an abstract

SNOWSHOE TYPES

There are nearly as many designs and shapes of snowshoes as there are climactic regions of North America, and choosing one can be as confusing as finding your way through a white-out blizzard. Here are some general factors to keep in mind as you make your choice:

● A large, wide snowshoe is the best choice for soft, deep snow because its greater surface area supports your weight on the snow surface more readily.

● A narrow snowshoe works best for traversing sidehills.

● A snowshoe with an upturned toe makes for the easiest downhill walking. Unlike a flat-toed model, the tips won't slide under the snow to cause a "face-plant."

● A snowshoe with a long tail "tracks" well, meaning that the tails help lift the toes out of the snow when you take a step. In deep soft snow, this aids in preventing you from catching a tip.

● A short snowshoe provides better maneuverability in negotiating tight timber or other obstacle-strewn terrain.

Most snowshoes combine these characteristics to varying degrees, but snowshoe expert Gene Prater (see Sources & Resources) divides them into four basic categories: the *Yukon*, the *beavertail*, the *bearpaw*, and the *Western*.

Of the four types, the Western has perhaps enjoyed the most popularity since its introduction in the 1950s, as the first shoe to replace the traditional steamed and bent white-ash frame and raw cowhide webbing with an aluminum frame and a nylon "deck."

Developed for mountain travel, the Western's design offers a compromise. It's fairly small and narrow, making it especially good for climbing in mountain terrain and on firmer snowpacks. The shape requires little modification in your normal walking stride, and it includes the metal cleat underfoot that clings securely to steep slopes.

The disadvantages of the Western crop up in very soft, deep snow, such as you might encounter in the North Woods; its small surface area may not maintain your weight above the surface. Likewise, its upturned toe can make it difficult to kick steps into the hard crusts that cover eastern mountains. Here many veteran snowshoers prefer to stick with their tried-and-true bearpaws and Yukons.

Snowshoe shapes: 1) a hybrid, called the Green Mountain bearpaw, works well in many conditions; 2) the Yukon, a traditional shape, has a long tail to aid "tracking" in deep powder; 3) the Western style is probably the most popular of all; 4) an asymmetrical model designed for racing; and 5) a Western shoe designed for kids.

painting or a bamboo forest. The snow was deep enough to cover all the underbrush. Essentially, we were walking above the forest floor, a great advantage to snowshoeing. Molly said she can snowshoe places in the winter where she can't hike in summer, because the undergrowth and deadfall are too thick.

The dogs picked up an elk trail and for a time we followed the trench that the big animals had packed out in the snow. We noted where the elk had scraped and chiseled with their big teeth at aspen bark to chew the nourishment out of it. The dogs sniffed out the huge thighbone and shin of an elk that lay in the snow, scored by the teethmarks of other animals — coyotes, speculated Molly and John. Skadi, a trained avalanche rescue dog and the mother of the other two Labs, contentedly squatted in the snow to gnaw and crunch at the marrow of the elk bone. Part of the pleasure of snowshoeing is this feeling of closeness to the animal

world. At times, you'll even feel like an animal yourself, winding through the silent, wintry woods.

As we climbed higher up the mountain, the aspens gave way to Douglas fir and blue spruce, while the snow became powdery. Here the snowshoes demonstrated their versatility, remaining as buoyant as waterwings even on this lightweight surface.

"What are the advantages of snowshoes over cross-country skis?" I asked during a rest break.

"They require less talent, they're less expensive, and a cross-country skier can't maneuver through tight trees like a snowshoer," Molly replied. "Also, it's difficult to ski downhill on cross-country skis in dense forest, but it's easy on snowshoes."

Later, I had the chance to give it a try. We began by cutting across a fairly steep hill. Sidehilling is probably the most difficult maneuver on snowshoes because the shoes want to slant with the slope and slip away downhill. To counteract this tendency, you give them a little kick so they carve out a small flat step. Failing that, you can turn your body so you face uphill and sidestep across the slope, or on a diagonal across and down, with your metal cleat underfoot providing traction.

Finally, we headed toward home down the slope of a gulley. Here the snow lay quite soft and powdery, and

On snowshoes you can travel virtually anywhere on snow. Here a snowshoer explores Bryce Canyon National Park in Utah.

the slope tilted at about 35 degrees. Molly chose an area that was more open but still treed, as a precaution against avalanches. She set off ahead, running downhill as the snow flew up around her. It looked as if she were floating, or running in slow motion, or moving as you would underwater. It looked like great fun.

"It's like jogging in feathers," said John, and took off after her, with the dogs plunging and springing behind him.

Snowshoe racing is one facet of a recent surge in interest in this humblest of winter sports.

And then it was my turn to fly and leap and slide down the slope in giant footsteps. This was how the astronauts must have felt on the moon; suddenly unfettered from the bonds of gravity.

DOGSLEDDING
AND SKIJORING

Whether the dog, as the cliché has it, is really "man's best friend," it is certainly his oldest among members of the animal family. Dogs were the first creatures domesticated by humans, about 10,000 years ago. They provided companionship, protection by way of barked warning, and assistance in hunting. By at least 1000 B.C., they had also been trained by natives of the Far North to tow sleds.

Today the use of dogs as tow animals is considered by many the province of a select few, and is often misperceived as an imposition on the animals. But in the last 10 or 15 years, as more and more Americans have taken to the outdoors in both summer and winter, the sport has undergone a revival. Dogsledding is available to anyone through guided trips, and its less-well-known cousin, skijoring, is easily enjoyed by any person and her canine companion.

DOGSLEDDING

A trip to Greenland a few summers ago sold us for good on dogsleds as a superior and liberating mode of travel. We'd hired a local sledder to transport us from the Thule Inuit village of Qaanaaq, which sits on Greenland's northwest coast only 800 miles from the North Pole, across

What the native peoples in the Far North have long known is just beginning to be appreciated more widely among the rest of us: dogsledding is a superb way to travel over snow.

twelve small Greenlandic huskies out onto the ice and hitched them to his 5x12-foot freight sled in a pattern that was fan-like, as opposed to the harnessing of dogs in the two-by-two column that most people picture from observing on television such organized dogsled events as the famous Iditarod race. Thomas's dogs tugged and pulled, eager to run, but were held fast by a "snow hook," a device like a boat anchor planted behind the sled to prevent overly zealous teams from sprinting away with a driverless sled.

Thomas released the snow hook and the sled jumped forward on heavy wooden runners sheathed in a Teflon-like plastic. The dogs spread out as they reached a trot, their paws flip-flopping merrily before us. Dressed in our full winter gear against the chill wind, we settled back comfortably on the warm caribou skins that covered the sled platform like pillow covers on a living room sofa.

"Harruck! Harruck!" Thomas shouted to the dogs.

They veered sure-footedly through the maze of ice heaves and bergs that projected like broken teeth

frozen Whale Sound about 15 or 20 miles until we reached the "ice edge." Here, where the shelf of ice that rims the shore ends and the open sea begins, Inuit hunters were said to stalk narwhals with kayaks and harpoons, an activity we were eager to observe.

It was a sunny late-June day when we gathered on the blinding white ice in front of the Norwegian-style house of our guide, Thomas Kivioq. He led his yipping team of

Camping on the shore of Basswood Island, in Lake Superior. Part of the Apostle Island National Lakeshore, such islands make fine destinations for dogsledders; the frozen lake is akin to Arctic conditions farther north.

from the frozen sea, and we began to have the eerie sensation that the dogs knew where to go without being told. The dogs' certain instincts and stamina would later serve us well — for black storm clouds had begun to pile on the northern horizon.

The first Europeans who arrived in the Arctic quickly saw the advantages of dogsleds over footpower. The Canadian Mountie and Alaskan sourdough mushing through the snows soon became archetypes of the Far North. "Musher," meaning dogsledder, in fact derives from the French-American verb *moucher*, "to go fast." However, though we hate to disappoint readers old enough to remember the television show *Sergeant Preston of the Yukon*, we must note that the term "Mush!" is no longer used as a command to the dogs.

The dogsled remains in many ways superior to the internal-combustion engine as a means of winter travel, and Thomas told us that he much preferred a dog team to a snowmobile. Dogs don't break down far from home, won't run out of gas, can function in virtually any weather or on any surface condition, and don't make a racket that scares away game. Perhaps most important, dogs, unlike snowmobiles, have enough brains to stop at the edge of *aineqs*, the wide cracks that split the sea ice.

We might add to Thomas's list that dogsleds make a perfect way for less-active people to experience the

Racing on Saranac Lake, New York. Middle-distance racing includes courses of from 15 to 150 miles and dog teams, like this one, of 14 dogs, although as many as 20 dogs are sometimes employed.

winter wilderness without the rigors of snowshoeing or skiing. Wrapped in caribou skins, Hudson's Bay blankets, or simply synthetic pile, you can lie back in a dogsled and watch the frozen wilderness glide by.

Sled-Dog Excursions

The International Sled Dog Racing Association calls dogsledding the "world's fastest growing winter sport," and while we'd argue that the claim is hyperbolic (we suspect the honor goes to snowboarding), interest is certainly booming. That interest is divided between those who breed, train, and race sled dogs and those interested in the purely recreational aspect.

A number of ski resorts, including Aspen, Colorado, and Banff, Alberta, offer guided dogsled trips (see Sources & Resources). You don't have to know how to drive a

dogsled (although your outfitter may teach you how); you merely sign on as a passenger on a ride that can last anywhere from one hour to several days, with the sleds driven by professional mushers.

Overnight accommodations range from spartan tents to luxury resorts with hot tubs and heated cabins. Whatever the lodging, you can expect hearty and well-prepared meals. See Sources & Resources for a listing of some dogsled tour operators in the United States and Canada, or try Chambers of Commerce or tourist offices near winter resorts to learn if sled-dog excursions are offered in the vicinity.

Hands-On Dogsledding

Raising, training, and racing sled dogs will appeal to those who love animals, and like to work closely with them. Make no mistake: sled dogs demand a lot of time, care, and love from their master. In return, however, they'll give you all the time and work and love that they have in them. It's this giving and receiving between master and dog team that make sled-dog running and racing an intimate and moving sport.

Types of Dogs

There is as much discussion among sled-dog drivers about breeding as there is among horse trainers. If you've never watched a sled-dog race, you might be surprised to see that not every dog is a husky. Many other breeds pull sleds, including Labradors, hounds, Irish setters, and non-purebred mixes. For racing, the most common sled dogs are the Siberian husky (by some accounts, the strongest animal for its weight in the world), the Alaskan husky, and a Labrador/hound mixture.

Nor is the biggest dog necessarily the best dog for pulling a sled. Noel K. Flanders, in her *Joy of Running Sled Dogs*, compares a 60-pound-plus dog like an Alaskan malamute or Lab to a draft horse that runs against a thoroughbred in the Kentucky Derby.

The bigger dogs excel at heavier loads, such as in weight-pulling contests and in long-distance running. For racing, most mushers prefer smaller dogs weighing under 50 pounds, including such breeds as the Alaskan or Siberian husky, Irish setter, and Samoyed.

Sled dogs come in all shapes and sizes, but among the most common is the Siberian husky (top and bottom). The Alaskan malamute (middle) is another popular pulling breed.

Sled-dog racers consider other factors besides size, such as long-leggedness and endurance. Leggy hounds make excellent sprinting dogs and can race along at up to 30 miles an hour for brief stretches, while Siberian huskies, for example, possess great stamina. Flanders says her team of Siberians maintains a pace of between 18 and 22 miles an hour on training runs.

A key part of the sled-dog anatomy is the feet, which must be able to endure miles of running over snow or ice. Adapting to the climate, the northern breeds have developed toes that nestle tightly together to prevent balls of snow or ice from

must be placed in their warm crates quickly after completing a course. Owners of long-haired dogs such as Irish setters also must trim the fur under the belly and around the legs so it won't collect snowballs. Mushers often tie little booties to their dogs' paws to protect them in sharp snow conditions.

Like many people who have never experienced it firsthand, we were under the vague impression that dogsledding might be cruel to the animals. But in your first moments in a dogsled, you cannot help but become convinced that these animals love to run. In fact, while you load a dogsled and attach the harnesses, you

The lead dog must be carefully selected and given special training so that it will properly steer the sled when given commands: *gee* for right, *haw* for left.

clinging between them. Likewise, their fur has evolved into a double coat, with a fine underlayer and a longer overcoat. The combination is so warm that these dogs perform best at around 10 degrees Fahrenheit, and may become overheated when temperatures climb higher.

On the other hand, single-coated breeds from southern climates can become chilled after a race. They

have to hold it in place with a snow hook like Thomas's to prevent the eager, yelping dogs and sled from taking off without you.

Still, it can be hard on dogs to run at a stiff pace for hours on end, and it is true that dogs have died of exhaustion during competition. Race organizers have taken measures to guard against injuring the dogs, and now require that teams stop at check-

A musher in Helena, Montana, lifts one of her dogs out of the dog house, a duplex condominium mounted on the bed of a pickup.

points where they are inspected by a veterinarian, who must certify that the animal is in good condition before it is allowed to continue.

Training a Dog Team

Marveling at the way the dogs towing our chartered sled responded to voice commands with the precision of the steering wheel of a car, we imagined a difficult, years-long ordeal plus a lot of luck and alchemy to bring a team to that level of performance. That time and commitment will pay off in a well-trained dog, but in fact, there's no more mystery to training a dog to pull a sled and respond to voice commands than to teach it to "sit" or "heel" or do other routine dog tricks.

The average dog is eager to learn; all it asks is that the trainer make clear what is required, and this does demand patience and commitment on the trainer's part. Like humans, dogs learn better when they are young; although many mature animals can be introduced to the harness, Flanders usually begins training when her dogs are three-month-old puppies. At this age, she fastens them to a small harness for a few minutes each day, with which they drag around a 10-inch length of two-by-four. As the puppy grows, it advances to towing a log, and is introduced to the commands "Hike" to move forward and "Whoa" to stop.

The next step is to tie the gangline (the line that attaches the dog to sled or logs) to a tree or stationary object and teach the animal to remain still, commanding "NO" if the dog tries to run. A perpetual problem with sled dogs is that once in harness, they are impatient to get going.

Flanders teaches the third key command, "On by," by running behind the dog as it pulls the log.

Gangline with harnesses laid out in readiness for the team of 12 eager dogs.

When the dog wishes to stop to smell an object or urinate on a tree, she orders "On by!" to deter the dog from such distractions and to keep it running down the track.

At this point in the training, Flanders suggests harnessing the dog to a bicycle and letting it pull you for rides on deserted roads, starting at a half-mile and working up to 2 or 3 miles per session. By the time you have three dogs trained to this point, you can use them to pull a cart, which you can build yourself or purchase from sled-dog outfitters (see Sources & Resources). As for an actual dogsled, a beginner can purchase a used model and related equipment for under $1,000.

To acquire a "steering wheel" for your team, you must next train a lead dog. Flanders chooses a dominant animal, ties it to logs to slow it down a bit, and runs along with it over a trail that includes forks. At first she runs ahead of the dog. When she approaches a right turn in the trail, she shouts "Gee, gee," and leads the dog to the right. The command for left is "Haw." Both words derive from the voice commands that teamsters used to shout to their horses.

After 3 or 4 days of taking the dog over the trail network, she lets the dog lead on its own and shouts "Gee" or "Haw" as they approach the trail's forks. She'll lavish praise on the dog if it makes the turn correctly.

Flanders advises that the trainer work the dog only 10 or 15 minutes at a time so it doesn't get bored, adding that the hardest part is often simply preventing the dog from wanting to run. For training variations, use your imagination. A friend of Flanders's shouted "Gee" or "Haw" as his dog routinely followed him around the house, and another trained his team to such precision

Finish line at a race on Lake Elmore in Lake Elmore, Vermont. Sled-dog racing is spreading far and wide in the lower 48 states.

that it could write his name in a field of snow by listening to his voice commands alone.

Sled-Dog Racing and Other Contests

If you have the opportunity to observe a sled-dog race firsthand, we strongly suggest you take advantage of it. It's a wild and joyous sport, especially at the starting line on a clear, cold winter morning, as the air resounds with the yips and barks of hundreds of eager dogs and the shouts of drivers as they attempt to hold them back.

At the signal, the drivers one by one release their snow hooks and the dogs sprint up the trail. The beauty with which the dogs work in tandem, and the deep bond between dogs and driver make for a moving and unique winter experience.

Over the last few decades, the sport of sled-dog racing has spread well beyond the Far North where it originated. Competitions are held in New England, the Midwest, and the

Rocky Mountain states from December to March each year. (For a schedule of races in your area or information about how to get started in sled-dog racing, contact the sled-dog associations listed in Sources & Resources.)

Races are held on specially prepared trails and sometimes on snowmobile or cross-country ski trails. In

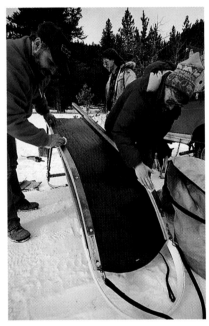

Two mushers treat the runners of their sled before the start of a race.

many parts of the country, snowmobile clubs will help pack out the dogsled trails in preparation for the races, although in a few places conflicts have occurred between dogsledders and snowmobile riders.

Races and other events are of several types:

● *Sprints*, the most common race, cover a distance of between 3 and 15 miles. Entrants are divided into the three-dog class, the six-dog class, and the eight-dog class. The latter may hit 28 miles per hour over a 10-mile course.

● *Middle-distance racing* includes races of from 15 to 150 miles by teams of six to fourteen dogs. Usually, teams run nonstop against the clock, but longer races include periodic stops at check-in stations to monitor the health of the dogs. Each must have the approval of a veterinarian before it can continue.

● *Long-distance races* can run from 250 miles up to the famous 1,160-mile-long Iditarod from Anchorage to Nome, Alaska. These include mandatory stops and layovers for the teams, food drops, and checkpoints, and en route drivers carry survival equipment. Besides the Iditarod (see pages 49-50), other well-known long-distance races include the John Beargrease 350 in Minnesota and the Governor's Cup 500 in Montana.

● *Peewee sled-dog racing* for children brings the whole family into the sport. Peewee racers run teams of as few as two dogs.

● Still another sled-dog competition is called a *weight pull*. This amounts to the canine version of a tractor pull. Dogs of different breeds and weight classes tow a "sled" loaded with concrete blocks or bags of dogfood (and sometimes equipped with wheels if

Unlike snowmobiles, sled dogs can find their way home under almost any conditions, including intense cold and blinding snow.

the site lacks snow) along a 16-foot chute. The power of the dogs and the weights they can pull are staggering: In 1986, a golden mastiff named Sam, owned by Dave Larsen of Laurel, Montana, pulled a sled weighing 3,130 pounds the length of the course in 9.23 seconds.

In our own experience, the dogsled proved itself once and for all

THE HISTORIC IDITAROD TRAIL

The myth persists that the Iditarod Trail Sled Dog Race, the world's most famous, commemorates the 1925 "Race for Mercy," in which a relay of sled-dog drivers covered a 674-mile stretch of Alaskan wilderness in 4 days to deliver desperately needed diphtheria antitoxin to Nome. In fact, the actual Iditarod Trail was farther south, significantly longer, and had been used by Athabascan natives long before the arrival of Russian explorers and traders starting in the 1700s.

The trail saw its heaviest use during the first decade of this century, when gold miners flooded into the territory. Actually a network of routes totaling about 2,200 miles, it was the only way to travel from the ice-free port of Seward to the gold camps around Nome.

In 1908, Allan Alexander Allan, a Scot considered one of the best drivers in the gold camps, organized a race from Nome across the Seward Peninsula to the tiny town of Candle and back, a
continued on next page

distance of 408 miles. The then-astronomical sum of $10,000 was offered in prizes.

The first Iditarod race in the modern series was organized in 1967 by Dorothy Page, an amateur historian, to commemorate the centennial of the purchase of Alaska from Russia. The race over the present trail, held every year since 1973, begins at the city of Anchorage, though the first leg ends after only 20 miles at Eagle River. There the dogs are trucked 30 miles farther north to Wasilla, where civilization begins to thin and snow cover to thicken. The total distance covered to Nome is actually 1,161 or 1,163 miles long, because different spurs are used in alternate years.

The Iditarod is an epic undertaking suitable only for the hardy and committed. Some racers have "stables" of as many as 200 dogs, and the costs associated with participation can run over $30,000.

One indicator of the experience and dedication required is that no non-Alaskan placed first until 1995, when Doug Swingley, a rancher from Simms, Montana, reached Nome in a record-breaking 9 days, 2 hours, and 42 minutes. His prize was $52,500 and a new pickup truck.

---

when a blizzard descended on our little party on the sea ice far off the coast of northern Greenland.

As the dark clouds rolled down from the north late that first day, Thomas aimed the sled toward a rocky island that protruded from the frozen sound. He threw chunks of seal meat to the dogs; they gobbled them down and curled up on the rocky beach to sleep off their feast. We humans pitched our tents — and found ourselves holed up for two days while the wind howled and snow pelted the thin fabric.

Thomas occupied himself with mugs of hot tea, long naps, and periodic trips up a hillside to scan the ice with binoculars. Finally he declared that we must turn back; the relentless north wind could break up the ice and we'd be surrounded by open water, and stranded.

We packed up and set off during a lull in the storm. Though confident in Thomas, we could not help feeling a bit of apprehension. Several times *aineqs* blocked our path, but with a pole Thomas maneuvered big chunks of ice to form a bridge. The dogs gingerly padded across the stepping stones of ice, and the long

While far less well known than most winter sports, skijoring is easy to learn, requires little equipment, and is good exercise for all involved.

sled managed to span several floes at once. A heavier, shorter snowmobile, we're quite sure, would have sunk straight to the bottom — and taken us with it.

Soon the storm closed in again and a heavy fog reduced visibility to a minimum. Everything before us — the sky, the frozen snow-covered sea, the icebergs that leaped startlingly from the mist, the fog itself — was white, and we had no idea in which direction the village lay.

Yet somehow, without a compass — or at least the kind of compass we know — Thomas and the dogs kept a straight heading. Nine solid hours of dogsledding later, the village of

Qaanaaq loomed reassuringly out of the mist. When we praised the dogs, we had the strongest feeling that they recognized, and appreciated, our gratitude.

SKIJORING

As we played tennis one sunny summer day, a young boy bicycled past the court, lazing on his two-wheeler while a leashed Alaskan husky pulled him merrily along. Impressed, we interrupted our serve and yelled, "Hey, how'd you teach him to do that?"

Deadpan, the kid replied, "I told him it was a sled."

SKIJORING ETIQUETTE

You may be able to obtain permission to skijor in areas not used by other winter outdoorspeople, such as a golf course or a private meadow, but more likely you will be sharing with cross-country skiers, hikers, horseback riders, and even bikers and snowmobilers. Among each of these groups, you will occasionally encounter an individual who takes it for granted that anyone who happens to choose a different sport from his is naturally a source for conflict. This is more likely when dogs are thrown into the equation.

The first rule for avoiding conflict is to keep your dogs under control. It is your responsibility to keep them from harassing people, other dog teams, and big game.

In most situations involving right-of-way, your most prudent choice is to yield. When meeting others, move off the track and allow them to pass. This is mandatory in the case of horseback riders; your dogs may not be aggressive, but the horse doesn't know that.

If you've ever been ambling peacefully along only to be startled by a cry of "Track!" followed by a hotshot cross-country skier shooting past your ear, you're aware of the unpleasant aftertaste this maneuver leaves in the mouths of slower recreationalists. Instead, make your presence known in gentler terms, and ask permission to pass.

The most common and valid objection to dogs on trails involves their droppings. Avoid contributing to a tarnishing of skijoring's image by adding a Ziploc bag and a garden spade to your pack.

He might also have told him it was a pair of skis. Skijoring, a pleasant way of snow touring as well as a competitive sport, is becoming increasingly popular with both humans and dogs in this country.

Skijoring began in Scandinavia in about the 1850s as a hybrid of dogsledding and skiing. Like many Europeans, the residents of Scandinavia were attracted to the various gold rushes of the western United States in the mid-nineteenth century. In this country they saw dogsledding, derived from the traditions of the Native Americans of the Far North, for the first time.

But back home in their more densely populated nations, keeping large numbers of dogs was impractical. Instead, Scandinavians used from one to four animals to pull a smaller and lighter sled called a *pulk*, or *pulka*, that was used only for carrying cargo. The driver, instead of riding, held on and skied behind. Nordic-style mushing, as this became known, is still popular in Norway, for sport, racing competition, and rescue work.

In the late nineteenth century, Americans took skijoring to its present form by abandoning the sled altogether. This provided a practical method of transport for professions involving gear that could be backpacked during relatively short day trips. Trappers skijored to check snare lines, miners skijored from camp to claim, and rural mail carriers skijored on their rounds.

Skijoring began in Scandinavia as a hybrid of dogsledding and skiing; instead of pulling a sled the dogs simply pull a ski-clad person.

Skijoring, while still lesser known than many winter activities, is easy to learn and a fun alternative method of backcountry locomotion. It requires little equipment and is good exercise for all involved.

As with any new activity, you'll

get the hang of it more quickly under the tutelage of a person with some experience, but you can certainly teach yourself, too. Start by ordering a copy of *Skijor with Your Dog*, by

Any fit dog weighing over 35 pounds can pull an average-sized adult on skis. Breed is less important than training, according to the experts.

the rudiments of the sport.

The skis can be standard touring models (most often used), alpine skis, or shorter versions of either. In addition to the harness handlebar, you might wish to carry ski poles for greater equilibrium and to aid the animals' efforts in deep snow or when going uphill.

Choosing and Training Skijoring Dogs

Most physically fit dogs weighing over 35 pounds can pull an average-sized adult on skis over moderate terrain. Breed is less important than train, and Høe-Raitto and Kaynor offer extensive advice on the latter.

Mari Høe-Raitto and Carol Kaynor (see Sources & Resources), an excellent and comprehensive manual.

Gear

The only specialized item you'll need is a harness that fits a dog or a small team, connected by a line about 4 feet long to a waist belt worn by the 'jorer, and equipped with a handlebar that helps you maintain balance and control. A typical kit, offered by the Piragis Northwoods Company (see Sources & Resources), is adaptable to one or two dogs and includes the harness, belt, a tow-bar system, and a pamphlet presenting

In general, skijoring commands and the methods of teaching them are the same as those used in dogsledding. "On by," however, takes on somewhat greater importance, since it is easier for a single animal or a two-dog team to stop to investigate some object than it is for a dog harnessed to a dozen of his fast-moving brethren.

Note that dogs, like humans, have preferences and dislikes.

who don't like to pull. Trying to force the animal to do so is frustrating for you and no fun for the animal.

Animal Care

Except in their most advanced years, dogs generally enjoy and benefit from exercise. To make it

All but the oldest dogs respond very favorably to the vigorous exercise of pulling. Still, make sure to watch your animals closely for signs of fatigue, and provide plenty of water and an extra ration of food, especially on a cold day.

Within any breed, even the husky or malamute, there will be individuals

pleasurable and safe, you'll wish to take the same precautions you

HORSEPOWER

The spot was perfect: a stretch of snowpacked logging road with 3-foot snowbanks plowed on each side, wending through a powdery high-mountain meadow. My friend Bill Vaughn walked Strider, a tall leggy eight-year-old red-roan gelding, from the trailer, while I tied 50 feet of rope to a plastic saucer-type sled. Bill wrapped several turns of the other end around his saddle horn.

I sat on the disk, Buddha fashion, and just managed to clutch the grab loops before the big horse took off, accelerating

down the road from zero to 25 miles per hour in a heartbeat. I piled into the snowbanks the first few tries, but before long, I learned to shift weight deftly enough to make banked turns up and down the berms.

Now I got out my metal-edged Telemark skis, untied the saucer, and knotted the rope to a foot-long length of 1-inch dowel. Soon Strider was plunging across the meadow as the powder billowed halfway to his chest, with me in tow, crouching for speed, "jumping the wake," and even "getting air" off a hummock or two.

continued on next page

We hadn't invented a new sport; we subsequently learned that when skijoring was introduced in this country before the turn of the century, its enthusiasts almost always used horses rather than dogs. The reason is obvious; at that time in rural areas, almost everyone owned horses, and most were already trained to pull a plow or carriage.

Horse skijoring is well within the skill of an intermediate skier. Aside from the obvious wisdom of keeping your tips up, it requires not much more than the ability to maintain a parallel position, and if you wish to hot-dog a bit, a confident turn.

As with dogs, you'll wish to pay attention to the experience and needs of your tow animal. The horse should be strong, long-legged, and accustomed to pulling a relatively heavy weight. Strider was trained for rodeo calf-roping, and had spent a lot of time dragging in deadfall firewood. There was no question that he was enjoying plunging through the deep stuff with us hanging on.

Snow for this activity must be either powder or packed without being icy. Wet snow will ball up painfully within the horse's shoes, and the horse will overexert in the pulling; too-slippery surfaces are dangerous to animal and rider alike. Finally, when sport is over, blanket your horse and walk it until its cardiovascular rate is normal.

---

would with a human companion, though to different degrees.

Pay attention to your dog's attitude; it isn't difficult to determine by demeanor when a dog is frisky, lethargic, thirsty, or worn out. Under more extreme skijoring conditions such as cold weather or racing, your dog may benefit from booties or a coat, and after heavy exertion, an extra ration of quality food may be in order.

For dog-care products, consult the advertisements in racing-specific magazines, such as *Mushing* and *Team & Trail* (see Sources & Resources).

S N O W B O A R D I N G

Not too many years ago, snowboarding was the oddball newcomer to the slopes. Traditional alpine skiers disdained it as the province of young "outlaw" riders who were, at best, reckless menaces. A joke of the time went: How does a boarder introduce himself to a skier? The answer: "Sorry, dude."

Today, skiers and snowboarders have learned to coexist cordially. Fewer resorts bar boarders from their runs, and increasingly snowboarding has become a mainstream — even family — sport. Its appeal embraces everyone from middle-aged skiers who want a new challenge to kids who might scorn skiing but who think boarding looks cool to city skateboarders eager to put their sidewalk skills to the test on the slippery surfaces of winter.

While most activities we describe in this book shun ski areas and their crowds, we simply couldn't resist including snowboarding. For several winters we watched curiously from the chairlift as boarders swooped beneath us.

We recognized something particularly graceful about those long carved turns, and elegance in the single board instead of the two planks that began to feel clumsily attached to our feet. We were envious of the way the boards

bruises one inevitably incurred during the first attempts.

This pain/gain trade-off was on our mind not long ago as we drove into the Sangre de Christo Mountains on the way to New Mexico's Santa Fe Ski Area. We stopped to pick up a young hitchhiker with a snowboard perched on his shoulder, and as we proceeded on, turned the conversation to the newly minted sport. When he waxed rhapsodic, we decided we would try it that very afternoon.

Alpine snowboarding involves carving turns down a slope, whether a typical downhill run, a race course, or a long powder run. And it can mean being airborne off a backcountry cornice.

glided easily over chopped-up powder and heavy "junk" snow that would send a skier sprawling. Besides, with all our ski experience to help us, snowboarding *looked* so easy, despite the stories about the

"Your butt's going to be sore tomorrow," our passenger remarked. This was not reassuring, yet now we were determined to pick up the gauntlet. "But it's easier to learn than skiing," he added.

Our young friend was right on both counts. It wasn't just our rear end, but also our wrists, elbows, back, and head that were sore the next day. After a lifetime of comfortably sliding down snowy slopes on skis and sleds, we felt like a child learning to walk who toppled every few steps and clonked to the ground with a grunt. The gentle slope looked terrifyingly steep, the lift towers looked unavoidable, and the clumps of skiers standing on the slope scattered when they saw our careening, arm-waving, uncontrollable approach.

But, to our surprise, after only two or three runs the awkward board felt more comfortable underneath our quivering legs. Once or twice — almost by accident — we actually carved a turn. We'd experienced just a tiny taste of that addictive, low-leaning swoop and whoosh of the snowboarder. Ignoring the bruises, we got back on the lift to try it again.

ALPINE VS. FREESTYLE

Snowboarders divide themselves into two broad camps, although you'll find all sorts of overlap between the two. Freestyle snowboarders are the tricksters and contortionists of the winter world. They're happy on an open slope but most at home in a "half-

A freestyle snowboarder performs a perfect toe-edged grab. Descended from skateboarders, freestylers are the tricksters of the sport.

pipe," a wide sloping ditch carved out of the slope that is something like the bottom portion of a giant conduit. Like skateboarders on a ramp, the freestylers shoot up the side of the tube and launch upward to catch air, flipping and spiraling in configurations with names like "alley-oop," "shiftie," and "720."

Freestylers can perform maneuvers on a regular open slope, too, doing "wheelies," "fakies," and "ollies." These are some of the basic

Mid-air maneuvers like this clearly set freestyle snowboarders apart from downhill skiers, as does the funky clothing they don.

Alpine snowboarding is the boarder's equivalent of alpine skiing. At its most basic, it involves cutting turns down a slope — whether it's a basic ski slope, a mogul field, a backcountry powder run, or a race course. Here the turns resemble more closely the carved turn of a skier.

The Board

You might think of a snowboard as a cross between an alpine ski and a surfboard, or as a very fat alpine ski. It traces its origins to a sliding device called a "Snurfer" that appeared in the 1960s and consisted of a simple board with a tether rope attached to the tip, which you held on to for all you were worth while you careened downhill.

By about the early 1980s, pioneers such as Tom Sims, Jake Burton Carpenter, and Demetre Malovich were designing boards that incorporated the properties of an alpine ski, enabling them to turn easily.

Like a ski, the tip and tail of a snowboard are wider than its narrow waist, a design aspect known as "sidecut."

A snowboard works in much the same manner as an edged ski. When you tilt the board to make a turn and the weight of your body presses down against the board's center, the board bends like a bow. This bending property causes the board to carve an arced turn as the steel edges cut into the snow surface like a knife.

maneuvers on which to build the fancier tricks. A wheelie resembles the same maneuver on a bike, but in this case you rock back and rear the front of your board off the snow. A fakie simply means riding backward. To perform an ollie, you jump the board into the air.

You then can advance to aerial tricks: for example, a toe-edged grab (gripping one side of the board as you fly) or, with enough experience, a "180-to-fakie," where you launch into the air, spin around, and land backward.

But we weren't much worried about learning new tricks. We began with the more straightforward style of snowboarding known as *alpine*.

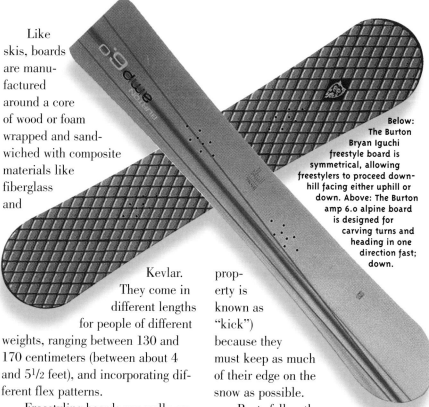

Like skis, boards are manufactured around a core of wood or foam wrapped and sandwiched with composite materials like fiberglass and

Kevlar. They come in different lengths for people of different weights, ranging between 130 and 170 centimeters (between about 4 and 5 1/2 feet), and incorporating different flex patterns.

Freestyling boards generally are "softer," meaning they flex, or bow, more easily when you press on the center. This allows the boarder to spin radically on the snow and otherwise perform his tricks. To help them turn more quickly, freestyle boards rate low in "swing weight," the effort it takes to rotate the board when a rider jumps into the air, and are designed with a turned-up tail and tip so the boarder can travel backward unimpeded.

Stiffer boards are used for alpine boarding or racing. They have less tendency to distort or skip when put on edge while carving at higher speeds. Their tails don't turn up (this property is known as "kick") because they must keep as much of their edge on the snow as possible.

Boots follow the same formula — freestyle riders use soft boots for maximum maneuverability, while alpine riders sometimes (but not always) wear a more rigid plastic boot that resembles regular alpine equipment, which aids in precise control on hardpack. Soft boots, and freestyle riding generally, have become more popular among American riders, many of whom come from a skateboarding tradition. Hard boots and alpine-style riding are more common in Europe, with its deep tradition of alpine skiing.

The original soft boots were "Sorel"-type rubber boots with leather uppers and felt liners for warmth, but now soft boots are made specifically for boarders. Soft boots require a "highback" binding; this amounts to a plastic tongue that runs partway up the calf. When you're wearing soft boots, this tongue gives you extra leverage for controlling the edge of your board that is cutting into the slope. Due to their rigidity, hard boots don't need this tongue of plastic; instead, a hard boot fits into a simple plate-type binding similar to a ski binding.

In alpine skiing your legs can flail wildly in different directions when you fall, so skis are equipped with elaborate release mechanisms to set free your foot and prevent a broken leg. Snowboard bindings do not have to release because your feet are, in effect, bound together in a single unit; in this configuration, your legs are less prone to injury, because in a fall they cannot be pried apart, so you avoid being turned into a human wishbone.

The most common snowboarding traumas involve upper extremities and include sprained wrists, thumbs, and fingers, all usually caused by catching yourself with your open hands when you fall. One way to help avoid hand injuries is to form a fist as you go down; wearing thick padded mittens is prudent.

Some boarders also don knee pads, and during the learning

1) The stiff alpine snowboarding boot is similar to a downhill ski boot. 2) Soft insulated boots based on the Sorel-style winter boot are made for freestyle snowboarding. 3) The latest innovation in snowboard footwear, this linerless lightweight boot is described by Burton as a "waterproof sneaker."

Notice the hard boots worn by this alpine snowboarder. Below: A freestyle binding designed to comfortably fit many styles of soft boots and provide unhindered freestyle mobility.

process, rear-end padding will also reduce bruising.

All boards come with a leash that you clip around one leg to prevent the board from running downhill without you, and a "stomp plate." This consists of a friction pad that sits between the front and back bindings. When on the flats or getting on or off a lift, boarders propel themselves by removing the rear foot from its binding and pushing along with it as you would on a skateboard. The stomp plate is where you place that free foot when you glide downhill (as off a chairlift ramp) for a short distance.

Heading Up, Boarding Down

The most disconcerting part of the undertaking, we found, is the moment that you first clamp your feet into the snowboard bindings. Arriving at Santa Fe Ski Area, we hooked up with our friend and mentor, expert snowboarder Jason Rawley. When he snapped shut our bindings, we felt we were welded to a large, immobile steel plate. Wherever we went, that board was coming with us — whether we descended upright or in a less dignified position.

Accept this from the start: You *will* fall at first. A lot.

Yet it came as an encouraging revelation when Jason stood up on his own board on the flat top of the mountain, hopped into the air, and spun 180 degrees. He encouraged us to do the same, and we suddenly felt more comfortable on the board, and realized that we could actually maneuver this thing.

Jason eased us into it, showing us how to walk around with our front foot fastened and rear foot free until we were comfortable with the feel of the board. (For more introductory tips see "Beginning Exercises," below.)

"A board works best when it's on edge," Jason explained. "Most of the time you're turning and putting the board up on one edge or the other. When it's riding flat to the snow, as opposed to on edge, the board tends to wobble and you can easily catch an edge and trip."

Jason demonstrated the basic ways to turn a board in a skidded turn. Most of your weight is on your

---

BEGINNING EXERCISES

You can overcome the initial awkwardness of snowboarding — that steel-plate-welded-to-your-feet feeling — with the help of these exercises:

● Before attempting to slide downhill on a board, spend some time walking around on the flat with your front foot in the binding and your rear foot out. Push the board along until you get up speed, then glide with your rear foot on the stomp plate.

● Try "pivoting." Find a flat spot, put both feet in the board's bindings, and rotate your shoulders and hips to make the board swivel back and forth. This will help you get the feel of swinging your rear foot around in your first turns.

● Practice edge control by "sideslipping." Choose a short slope with a bit of pitch to it and slide down sideways with your toes pointing into the hill. Try to control the bite of your edge by rocking up on your toes so that you slide, stop, slide, stop. Climb back up again to try your "heel edge." Be sure to keep your knees bent when you do this maneuver.

● Start easy. When you're ready to board your first slope, choose the most gentle "bunny hill." Make your first descents straight down it, and as your balance and confidence build, try your first turns. By gradually building up to the steeper stuff, you'll save yourself a lot of falls.

---

forward foot while your back foot is used as a rudder to help steer you through your turns (see "Which Foot Forward?," below). To initiate a turn, you put your weight forward, lean into it, and bring the board around by pivoting that rear foot.

To make the board track straight, you simply move your weight to your rear foot and the back portion of the board.

Jason guided us down a few runs and gave us a few pointers about what we were doing wrong. Like a beginning skier, our instinct was to lean back when we should

This water-proof breath-able jacket includes a zip-out reversible, insulated vest and a removable hood.

T E C H N I Q U E   T I P

WHICH FOOT FORWARD?

Like surfers, some snowboarders ride "regular," with their left foot forward, and some ride "goofy-footed," with their right foot forward. Which is right for you doesn't necessarily correspond to whether you're right- or left-handed.

Snowboarders have devised all sorts of formulas and indicators to determine which foot to put forward and which to the rear. For instance, it's been suggested that your forward foot is whichever one you plant beside a ball when you are about to kick it. But all these tests boil down to one thing: personal preference. Try strapping on the board both ways, and go with whichever arrangement feels best.

Which foot you put forward will determine whether you face toward the left or right edge of the board. This also establishes which is the board's "toe edge" and which is its "heel edge." For a beginner, it's generally easier to make a toe-edge turn because you can control the board's tilt with the calf muscles.

The ultimate in alpine snowboarding — giant slalom racing.

got to work it out for yourself."

We pushed over to the chairlift and found another boarder standing in line — a woman about our own age, which is to say, nearly twice Jason's age.

"At first I couldn't go 20 feet without falling," she told us as we rode up the lift together. "But after a while, you know, I learned to stand up and go straight. Then one day I started turning. Now I've snow-boarded five or six times, and it's really getting to be fun."

Thus inspired, we threw ourselves into the job of learning to board in the school of hard knocks.

be pushing forward, with the result that we'd go flying along in a straight line without much control over the board's edges. But the basic principles of boarding, if not the actual performance, were surprisingly simple.

"I've taught you everything I can," Jason said when we reached the bottom of the slope. "Now you've

FUN AND GAMES

I n his 1911 tome *A Winter-Sports Book*, the British writer Reginald Cleaver notes that "the one decisive sign of old age [is] when a man prefers his professional work to his recreation, feels more interested in it, and gains from his successes in work more joy than from the fleeting triumphs of his play-hours. If any of my readers are haunted by a lurking suspicion that this description may be not wholly untrue of himself. . .let him go to Montana in the dead of winter."

The Montana to which Cleaver refers is not our home state, but a resort in the Swiss Alps about 20 miles north of Zermatt. There, and at spas such as Davos and St. Moritz, many of the 4,500 members of the Public Schools Alpine Club, mostly alumni of Harrow and Eton, gathered with their wives and children each winter. The basic goal was messing around on snow and ice — substances that lend themselves gloriously to exactly that.

Messing around is the key to gaining more joy from those fleeting winter play-hours, and "play" is the watchword. Many of the illustrations in Cleaver's book show harmless mishaps: folks slipping and sliding, being tossed from speeding sleds, face-planting on skis. Snow and ice are licenses to look foolish, because you'll look no more foolish than

the way to the sporting equivalent of the slapstick pie fight.

Some of the best winter activities allow adults and kids to compete together; the agility of children is the great equalizer when the playing field is snow or ice. You'll be the one slipping and sliding and trying to catch up to *them*, and they'll love it.

CROSS-COUNTRY TAG

Among our most vivid memories from the slapstick-yet-competitive

Messing around in snow might well begin with making a snowman. And what afternoon that begins with a snowman ever ends in anything short of a snowball fight?

anyone else. They offer you a rare moment in adult life to abandon your self-consciousness and simply have fun.

Not all of the activities in this chapter are pure frolic, but don't neglect the ones that are. Think of it this way: Winter play can range from serious, razor's-edge competition all

category are the games of "cross-country tag" we played after school. We'd get about twenty friends together, choose a snowy meadow or big lawn with some patches of woods nearby, designate some vague boundaries, and draw straws for who would be "it."

To start the game, the person who was "it" stood on cross-country

Don't allow the arrival of snow and ice to curtail your outdoor activities. The knobby-tired mountain bike is far better adapted to winter conditions than its slender-tired touring cousin.

skis at the bottom of a small, gentle knoll, and at the signal everyone else shot downhill en masse in his general direction. "It" usually managed to tag a few at this mass start; those who were tagged then would be enlisted to chase and tag others, often working in tandem to trap and cut off escapees like a pack of bloodhounds running down an escaped convict.

Finally, only a few skiers were left untagged, and that's when the game got truly crazy. We remember wild sprints on cross-country skis through the woods in manic flight from our rabid pursuers, skis flapping through the brush like great duck feet. We usually got caught because we ended up laughing so hard we collapsed in a heap.

Even better were the games of cross-country tag on full-moon nights. It was a more serene game, with the moon so brightly reflecting from the snow that you could see nearly as well as in daylight, as shadows flitted and glided and whispered through the woods.

For a more challenging version of tag that is best played on foot, stomp out a series of interconnected trails in the snow, such as a 100-foot circle bisected by other trails like a pie cut into slices. The participants are not allowed to leave the trails, which makes for wild chases up and down the pie sections and around the perimeter.

A few words of advice: First, don't wear your $500 racing skis. You have a tendency to run over logs and stumps and, once in a while,

Snow adds a new dimension to many games, including the tug-of-war. These combatants are on Mirror Lake in Lake Placid, New York, scene of many winter games.

someone's ski tips get stomped on while they are chasing behind an escapee. Second, the rules require that you use your hand rather than your ski pole to tag your prey. Otherwise it's too easy to stab someone with a tip.

HARE AND HOUNDS

I was eight years old when I first played this sport with my Uncle Dick, a passionate gamesman. I tracked him through the snow on a frigid January day, feeling quite proud of my scouting skills — until the bootprints doubled back on themselves and ended in a baffling loop. I pondered this impossibility for what

felt like a very long time, until a branchful of powder poured over my head and down my jacket. I looked up to spot Uncle Dick perched high overhead in an oak tree. I thought him very clever for that strategy.

The rules are simple: The "hare" gets a 5-minute head start (or count slowly to 100) and the "hounds" set off to track him through the snow to a hiding place. In a variation, the "hare" tries to loop back to the starting place before being caught.

Your strategy as the hare is to obscure by cunning means the tracks you leave in the snow. Walking backward in your own footprints is an elementary though time-consuming tactic; other excellent methods are climbing trees, hopping between exposed rocks, shinnying along post-and-pole fences, or walking on wind-cleared ice.

Hare and hounds can also be played on cross-country skis or snow-shoes; both make that last dash to the finish line more challenging. One precaution if the playing territory is large: Equip the hare with a marine-quality whistle that can be heard for at least a half-mile. The hare wants to get lost, but not permanently.

TUG-OF-WAR

Assemble teams by the tried-and-true "choose-up" method. The captains are appointed from the younger generation (providing for the humbling possibility that your own child may pick you last). Each captain must select an adult and then a kid alternately. A spare glove or handkerchief marks the center point, and the winning team is the one that yanks the lead tugger of the opposite side past the marker.

FLASH-FREEZING SUMMER SPORTS

You can adapt many of your favorite fair-weather sports to winter, and pursue them somewhat more recklessly. The best thing about playing in snow is that it is soft. You can fling yourself around with abandon, with less chance of damage to your old bones.

At the annual year-end party at our friend Annick Smith's ranch, the

ICE GOLF

For about a dozen years beginning in the early 1970s, various charitable organizations sponsored a golf tournament on snow-covered Foys Lake near Kalispell, Montana. Standard-sized cups were drilled into the frozen surface and fixed with regulation flags to form a nine-hole course rated par 27, with "fairways" shoveled down to bare ice.

John Gardner, tourney champ in 1984 with a one-over 28, told us that his memory of the event centers on three things: The longest hole was about 150 yards; it was mid-February; and it was darned cold. About fifty golfers turned out nonetheless, each limited to a putter and one other club; Gardner chose a nine-iron.

Gardner says the key to ice golf is keeping your shot out of the deep snow of the "rough," which tends to bring the ball to a stop in short order, and makes it hard to find as well. Any other tips for the budding ice golfer? "Wear a lot of clothes," Gardner replies, "and have some schnappes near to hand."

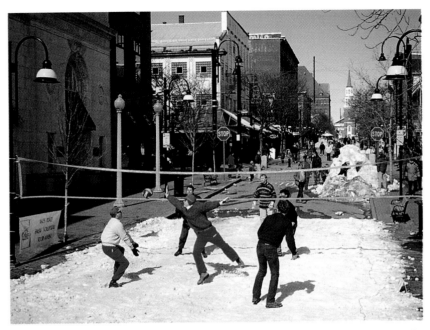

Soft powder snow may be ideal for volleyball, but even cruddy old snow will do, as these players in Burlington, Vermont, prove.

volleyball net comes out. Soon otherwise sober adults are flinging themselves face-first into shin-deep powder in pursuit of the sort of "dig" they haven't made since high school.

The morning of Super Bowl Sunday calls for the traditional snow football match. A ball fully inflated at room temperature will soften somewhat in the cold, making it easier to grip — at least at first. Under the right conditions the ovoid will ice up eventually, so pigskin pursuit becomes more like greased-pig pursuit.

February means it's time for the local Parks and Recreation's Snow Joke softball tournament, where "sliding into home" takes on a whole new meaning. The softball is spray-painted orange for visibility, although in our pickup games we use a regulation white model; for hilarity, little matches the sight of a right fielder pawing through the snow like a dog after a bone, seeking the elusive ball. Aluminum bats are advised, incidentally; the wooden variety can break if the day is cold enough.

SNOWBALL FIGHTING: THE MARQUESS OF QUEENSBERRY RULES

Remember the scene in *Butch Cassidy and the Sundance Kid* where a gang member challenges Butch to a knife fight? Butch accepts. "But first," he says, "we've got to discuss the rules." The gang member gawks at him in disbelief. "*Rules?*" he says. "In a *knife fight?*"

When we get off on the subject of rules in a snowball fight, people are similarly surprised. We'll grant that there are attractions to general chaos in this sort of battle — and we love a good free-for-all in the snow — but if, like us, you also have a competitive streak, sometimes you'll want a way to keep score.

Generally begun as random acts of harmless violence like this potshot at the photographer (by his son), the snowball fight can also be formalized into teams and score keeping.

The Marquess of Queensberry was the British nobleman who, in 1867, codified bare-knuckle brawling to turn it into the organized sport of boxing. Inspired by the Marquess some years back, we decided to similarly organize snowball fighting.

After the team captains choose up sides, it's time for construction of two snow forts. The distance apart, length, and height are a matter of group consent, and both forts should have about the same dimensions. A belly-button-high wall with 2 feet of protection per combatant makes a good general-purpose bulwark. Incidentally, the seasoned campaigner will direct his team to use the snow on the no-person's-land between the forts for the construction, for reasons that will soon become apparent.

With the combatants behind the protection of their forts, the battle begins at the timekeeper's signal. Points are made by hitting an opponent, but scores are highly subjective. The scorekeeper (yup, we've got one of those, too) has wide latitude in assessing form, style, splat factor, and whatever other whimsical criteria she has in mind on any given battle day. A grazed arm might be a "1," while a solid smack in the chest just as the opponent is about to launch a snow missile might rate as high as a "4."

For safety, snowballs cannot be made in advance of the commencement of battle, or be stockpiled during its course; packed snow tends to become painfully hard in short order. It is permissible, however, to assign one or more team members to "ammo" duty, forming the balls and passing them to the throwers. When this is done efficiently, a team can go from single-shot mode to semiautomatic rapid-fire.

Eventually, you'll begin to use up all the available snow in the area protected by your fort (now you see why you didn't expend it in building the structure). You've got two choices, both dicey. You can dart out to the side, hoping to grab up a double-armful to resupply without being nailed; or you can move to the rear. Either exposes you.

As the engagement progresses, the captains' choice of a well-balanced team becomes a crucial factor. The value of a "dodger" who can scavenge snow while eluding shots cannot be overestimated. You'll want a couple of "riflers" of course, strong-arm types who can pop up, zero in, and nail an exposed enemy. But an even more devastating weapon in your human arsenal is a "mortar." This is a person who has perfected the art of lobbing snowballs high into the air using an underhand slow-pitch/softball-type delivery, nullifying the protective value of the opponents' fort and raining destruction from above.

We require ski goggles for all combatants. You never know when you might get popped by sniper fire.

CALMING DOWN

Not all winter outdoorsing need be vigorous. The picnic is a pleasurable addition to a nature hike, a snowshoe trek, a sledding expedition, or a skating party.

A day-trip picnic offers creative culinary opportunities less available in camping, where weight is always a consideration. Whatever the size of the party, you can have all the luxuries of comfort and fine food with no one packing more than 10 pounds on his or her back.

A bright sunny day is probably the best choice for your first picnic, especially if children are included. You'll be surprised how warm you'll be even in temperatures well below freezing if the day is clear and windless. But less clement conditions can also host a perfectly pleasant winter picnic if you dress properly (see Chapter 14). During one April high-country outing we lunched on cheese, prosciutto, and fresh fruit in a whiteout blizzard. We ate in comfort because we'd anticipated the volatile weather conditions, although admittedly it was difficult to get the Brie to room temperature.

It's fun to pick a target destination before you set out: a nontechnical mountaintop, an alpine meadow, a frozen waterfall. (One of our goals is to find a picnic spot where you can ski and fly-fish on the same spring afternoon; needless to say, we're still looking for that one.) The luncheon is your reward upon reaching your goal. Don't be overly ambitious, and do be willing to change your plan if, for example, children become fatigued or crankily hungry, or the weather changes.

Time your return so you'll be back well before dark; depending on the terrain and the length of the hike, give yourself a buffer of 1 to 2 hours. As with all backcountry excursions, inform someone of where you are going and when you expect to be back — and remember to check in when you do return. More than one search-and-rescue team called out by a worried friend has spent a cold night in the mountains while the "lost" party was in fact gathered in a fireplace-

Trying to make an auto-size snow boulder is one way to work up an appetite for a winter picnic.

warmed living room, eating popcorn and watching M*A*S*H reruns.

When choosing our picnic spot, we try to find a bit of dry ground on which to sit. This might be a patch under an evergreen tree where little snow has fallen or has melted off; the grassy, dry south face of a steep hillside; a rock outcrop exposed to sun; or even a deadfall tree trunk. Short of dry ground, you can tromp out an area in the snow and lay down a tarp or space blanket, then place your empty pack or skis atop it for better insulation from the cold snow underneath.

You can start a campfire in the snow if you really want to get festive and warm. A hot drink can make all the difference between spartan and luxury conditions during a snow picnic; bring a thermos, or a small, lightweight camp stove and a pot in which to melt snow.

You'll be hungrier than you guessed when you eat in the cold, so don't stint on the portions. And we've found that we can never bring too many candy bars.

A gear list with sample menu for a winter picnic appears below, but here are three items that are particularly handy.

Pack petroleum jelly; a bit of grease on the face feels nice, especially when a breeze kicks up. If you'll be cooking on site, slip a square foot of $1/8$-inch plywood into your rucksack, for stability under your stove and to keep it from melting itself down into the snow. Finally, try forgoing the Mylar blanket in favor of self-inflating sleeping pads. While the former is lighter, more compact, and reflective, it results in distinct butt-chill without other padding. One mattress per two picnickers will suffice.

A PICNIC LIST

This list is for a party of six when the destination is no more than a couple of miles from the point of embarkation. For longer hikes, you might want to consider adding a first-aid kit and flashlight.

GROUP GEAR

3 self-inflating sleeping pads
3 small plastic trash sacks
Plastic or paper knives, forks, plates, cups, and napkins
Utility knife
Optionally: Pots, pans, stoves, and utensils, depending on your menu

PERSONAL GEAR

Petroleum jelly, sunblock lotion, and lip balm
Sunglasses
Camera and binoculars
Toilet tissue

A SIMPLE SAMPLE MENU

Appetizers: cheese and crackers
Soup: soup in Thermos
Main course: bread, cheese, cold cuts, condiments, pickles, fresh pre-sliced vegetables
Dessert: homemade pie, cake, or brownies
Beverage: soft drinks, coffee in Thermos

Bear in mind that alcoholic beverages, if you choose to imbibe, increase the body's susceptibility to hypothermia (see Chapter 15). And carry no glass — it's not only heavy, but broken glass in the snow will remain in spring as unsightly and dangerous litter. If any of your foodstuffs come off the shelf in jars, repackage in plastic containers.

THE NATURE OF SNOW AND ICE

Imagine that you grew up in Micronesia and have never seen snow, until one day you are shanghaied and dumped off in the middle of a Vermont meadow on a sunny January afternoon. What would you feel and sense?

First, you can barely open your eyes, because the snow is so painfully white in the bright sun. Second, your sandals sink into the fluff, and immediately the cold numbs you from the ankles to the tips of your toes. Third, when you try to walk, you slip and slide and get nowhere.

It is ironic that most people who have lived all their lives in snow country regard the substance with the same rudimentary conceptions: It's white, cold, and slippery. Yet snow comes in thousands of varieties, hundreds of shades and textures, and possesses a volatile — and fascinating — personality that can reinvent or disguise itself faster than a con artist working a country fair.

Consider snow cover as a living organism that constantly undergoes metamorphosis. It's actually not unlike a big sheet of bread dough that's been left to sit so the yeast can make it rise. From the outside it may appear plain and white and inert, but on the inside millions of changes occur every second.

On closer inspection, snow and ice — water's two winter guises — reveal many new faces beyond their sheer beauty and majesty.

DID YOU KNOW

The age-old question of whether every snowflake is unique has never been answered, and likely won't be. An average snowstorm produces around 10^{21} ice crystals — that's 10 followed by 21 zeros. To put this number in perspective, imagine taking one flake and comparing it to each of the others. Now imagine you had superhuman powers, and could process 1,000 flakes every second.
You'd complete your chore in a mere 31.7 billion years.

TYPES OF SNOW

One way to understand snow is to burrow down into that cover from the top and look around carefully as we go. Let's start with a frosting of snow from a recent storm — a delicate layer of light, new-fallen flakes. Skiers and other connoisseurs of snow generally call this *powder*; it's the type that most people generically picture as "snow."

If we pick up a handful, scatter it on a piece of black paper, and examine it with a magnifying glass, we'll usually discover tiny six- and twelve-pointed stars. They look like the "snowflakes" that grade-schoolers cut out of folded paper to decorate their classroom windows; to scientists they are known as "stellar crystals." In certain conditions, however, we might instead discover tiny needles or columns or plates of ice.

A snow or ice crystal forms when a speck of dust enters a cloud of "supercooled" water vapor and the molecules of water lock into rings of six molecules each and cling to the dust mote.

More and more six-sided rings join together and eventually grow into a crystal. That classic stellar crystal occurs when the temperature inside the cloud is around 5 degrees Fahrenheit (minus 15 degrees centigrade). Shapes like needles and columns occur when ice crystals form at lower or higher temperatures (see "Supercooled Water and the Facts of Ice," page 84.)

As it falls, the snow crystal sometimes sticks together with other crystals. While we use the term "snowflake" for crystals of all types, scientists reserve the word to describe this large bunch of stuck-together crystals. If that crystal falls through a particularly moist cloud, it will gather a layer of ice called "rime" that blurs its features or coats it so thickly that it bounces on the ground like a little Styrofoam ball. This type of snow is called *graupel*, meaning "granular" in

German. Some meteorologists refer to it as "soft hail."

But in this case, we watch as the stellar crystals build up in a feathery ground cover and stack delicately on tree limbs and fence posts. This new-fallen powder can be as little as 2 percent water and

At high altitudes, exposed to unrelenting wind, powder snow can become densely packed and tortured, resembling sandstone. In this form it is known to backcountry skiers as *sastrugi*.

98 percent air — known as "2 percent density snow" to researchers, and dubbed by skiers "cold smoke." The tiny arms of the stellar crystals hold each other at arm's length, like a pile of kid's jacks.

If a strong wind blows up and tumbles those snow crystals along the ground, however, it snaps off their arms. When they come to rest they'll pack cheek-to-jowl into a much denser snow texture called *windpack* or *sastrugi*. Eskimos call it upsik and slice it into blocks to build igloos.

Burrowing down into the snowpack past the upper layers of powder or windpack, we encounter other tex-

Burrowing beneath layers of fresh powder and into old layers of snow can tell the story of a winter's snowfalls. Here Telemark skiers head toward Mistaya Peak near Golden, British Columbia, Canada.

tures. Perhaps we strike a dense crust of ice that formed a few weeks earlier when the snow melted and refroze. If caused by a bright day, this is a "sun crust"; if resulting from liquid precipitation, it's a "rain crust." Breaking our way beneath, we might encounter a thick, crumbly layer that we can scoop up in big handfuls. This is *old* or *consolidated snow*.

Here the snow has "metamorphosed" over the weeks that it sat in the cold. The arms of each stellar crystal shrunk inward, like a yogi folding his limbs in on himself, until the snowflake transformed into a tiny knobbly ball of ice. Tiny necks of ice, known as *sinters*, then grew between each ball of ice. If you examine this kind of snow under magnification, it resembles glass

beads on a string.

Digging deeper still until we mine our way to the layer of snow closest to the earth, we find what's known as *depth hoar* or *sugar snow*. Mountaineers and backcountry skiers fear this type because it forms a weak layer in the snowpack that can collapse and cause avalanches when the weight of more snow piles atop it. Depth hoar forms when a sharp temperature difference exists between the warm earth underneath the snowpack and the frigid air on top. This often occurs during early-season cold snaps when the snow cover is thin and not much distance separates the warm earth from the cold atmosphere.

Over time, these near-ground crystals vaporize and travel upward to the colder layers. There the vapor refreezes on existing crystals and transforms them into distinctive cupped and ribbed formations, some of which look like tiny Great Pyramids under a magnifying lens. Unlike consolidated snow, no sinters of ice hold

Firnspiegel meaning "glacier mirror," is a thin, clear sheet of ice that forms over the snow on bright sunny days accompanied by cold temperatures.

these distinctive crystals together. Instead, the texture of depth hoar is loose and granular like a handful of sugar. It can and does slip off a mountainside, sometimes suddenly and massively.

You won't necessarily find these types of snow in the same order as you burrow into the snowpack. Whatever arrangement or types of snow you do find, read them like an archaeologist reads earth strata and you'll learn the "history" of the winter.

Snow in Old Age

The warmer temperatures of spring bring massive changes to the snowpack and obliterate the subtle layers that tell the winter's history. The same warm days and cold nights that cause the sap to flow in maple trees trigger a "melt/freeze cycle" in the snowpack. During the days the smaller snow crystals thaw, and at night the meltwater refreezes onto

larger crystals.

In effect, the larger crystals get bigger and the small crystals vanish. In your hand, this type of snow looks like rock salt. In the Alps it is called *sulzschnee*; American skiers call it *corn snow*. It usually makes its appearance about mid-March in much of the northern United States and marks the advent of shirtsleeve and suntan weather. Its firm surface is ideal for all sorts of snow activities, from skiing to sledding to glissading. The best conditions are between late morning and early afternoon, when the sun has softened up the top inch or two but before it becomes too slushy.

Odd Snow: *Firnspiegel* and Its Cousins

We've all heard the cliché that Eskimos have 27 or however many words for snow. Certainly skiers, climbers, and snow researchers have added at least that many names to

When ice crystals collide with supercooled droplets of water, the droplets freeze onto the crystals. The crystals become coated with a layer of frozen droplets, called rime.

light up in the phenomenon known as "glacier fire." Tromping through firnspiegel is a satisfying experience; it sounds as if you are walking on — and in the process shattering — plates of fine china.

Surface hoar is delicate feathers of frost that grow on top of the snow during cold clear nights, when water vapor condenses out of the air like dew on a summer night. Sheets of surface hoar form on the walls of your non-frost-free freezer if you leave the door shut for several weeks.

the vocabulary. Here are a few of the odder types:

Firnspiegel is roughly translated from the German as "glacier mirror," and describes a thin skin of ice that forms over the snow under a rare combination of warm sun and cool breezes. The layer of firnspiegel reflects evening and morning sunlight so that whole mountainsides

Pukayaaq is the type of snow that the Inuit of Baffin Island prefer to melt for drinking water. It was described to us by Aksayuk Etuangat, a ninety-two-year-old elder, as "icy snow which is not frozen" that has been exposed to the sun. In other words, it's snow that's high in ice and water content instead of air, not unlike our "corn snow."

Suncups are pockmarks that appear in high-mountain summer snowpack after the sun has beat down for several days. These resemble the dimples on a giant golf ball. A similar phenomenon, *wind-cups*, is formed by warm breezes.

Penitent snow owes its name to Spanish-speaking explorers of the Andes Mountains, who likened its drooping cones to atoning sinners. These cones appear only at high altitude in the tropics. The relentless equatorial sun melts deep pockets in the snow, leaving pillars that present minimum surface area to the sun's heat and can stand as tall as 10 feet.

Snow rollers or *cinnamon rolls* are spontaneous snowballs that occur when a bit of snow drops from, say, a tree branch, and then rolls downhill gathering accumulating layers like a spiral pastry. For this to happen, the snow must be "sticky" (see "Why Snow Sticks," page 88).

Diamond dust refers to snowflakes that fall mysteriously from a cloudless winter sky, sparkling in the sunlight as they descend. They form when a layer of warm moist air slips over the top of colder air hugging the ground. The water vapor then condenses out of the blue sky into snow crystals.

THE MYSTERY OF ICE

I grew up on the shore of a Wisconsin lake, and every autumn I eagerly awaited that cold, still November night when the sun set on the water's surface and I awakened to a smooth, shimmering sheet of ice. The transformation seemed magical, and I wondered at its suddenness.

What I didn't know was that the lake had been preparing for the moment for months.

How a Lake Freezes

Starting around September, as the sun dips lower in the southern sky, a lake begins to lose its heat into the colder air. Eventually the surface reaches a temperature of 39.2 degrees Fahrenheit (4 degrees centigrade), at which water is most

DID YOU KNOW

Ski areas manufacture snow by blowing a mixture of air and water through compressed-air guns. To encourage snow formation, the mix often contains an additive — harmless, dead bacteria called *Pseudomas syringae*. This organism, originally discovered on the leaves of frost-damaged corn, contains a protein whose structure resembles an ice crystal and acts as a nucleus to encourage water to freeze at warmer temperatures.

dense. The surface water sinks to the bottom, displacing warmer water which rises to cool in its place.

This circulation of water is called "overturn." Besides promoting freezing, it distributes surface oxygen and food to fish and other deep-dwelling aquatic life before the ice seals them in for the winter.

Once the whole lake has reached a temperature of 39.2 degrees, it's ready to freeze. One of the bizarre properties of water is that when it turns to a solid — ice — it expands in size by about 10 percent. This is because the water molecules in an ice crystal form a lattice-like pattern that spaces them farther apart than in their liquid form. Most liquids, in contrast, *contract* when they freeze to a solid. This is why ice forms on top

DID YOU KNOW

Snow appears white because its surface reflects much of the sunlight. Ice and snow particles are of such a structure that they absorb or block out the red colors of the spectrum but they act as if transparent to the blue colors and allow them to pass deeper into the snowpack. That's why the sides of a deep hole dug in the snow will look blue.

of a lake instead of sinking to the bottom — it's a little bit lighter than water.

Our grandfather, who loved to skate and iceboat, marveled at this phenomenon. Each winter he explained to us kids that if ice *sunk*, the continents would flood annually, and human life never would have evolved. He told it vividly, and though we'd heard the story often, the enormity of the ramifications never failed to transfix us.

After overturn has brought the water to a uniform 39.2 degrees, surface cooling continues until the temperature drops to the freezing point. Now ice crystals begin to form around a nucleus, perhaps another ice crystal or a speck of mineral.

Supercooled Water and the Facts of Ice

We've all been taught that water freezes at 32 degrees, but in fact it is not absolutely true. A droplet of pure water needs a temperature of minus 40 before it will solidify. To freeze at higher temperatures, water demands a nucleus around which to form an ice crystal.

In "supercooled" clouds of vapor, such as those that drift high above a winter landscape on a December day, water freezes around motes of dust and clay, and sometimes even minute specks of meteor. Some of these nuclei, which are mainly silicate minerals, cause water vapor to freeze at warmer temperatures than others. The

That lakes freeze over quite suddenly is no accident. They prepare for the moment for months, as the water cools toward the magic number 39.2 degrees F.

crystals grow into plates and needles at cloud temperatures near freezing, and fall as the classic "stellar" snowflakes when the cloud temperature hovers just above zero.

Water *will* freeze at 32 degrees when crystals of ice are already present, providing another form of nucleus around which more ice can form. These types of crystals begin as disks a few millimeters in diameter. Providing the night is windless, the disks join into a smooth sheet, sometimes called black ice. The ice slowly thickens on its underside by forming "candles" — long, hexagonal crystals about as thick as your little finger, and joined side by side.

The ice surface expands and contracts with changes in temperature, which triggers all sorts of strange occurrences on a frozen lake. Expanding ice is inexorably

DID YOU KNOW

About four-fifths of the country receives enough cold each winter to drop water temperatures to the freezing point, and in fully one-quarter, lakes are on average ice-covered for 100 days or more.

Swift-moving water in streams hovers around 32 degrees and forms into disks called "frazil ice." When such disks stick to the bottom they enlarge to become "anchor ice."

up like pieces of crumpled cardboard.

During nights of below-zero cold, the ice sheet may suddenly contract with a haunting boom that echoes up and down the lake. The ice can crack and shift under your feet. I used to stand on the ice on evenings like this and wait for these booms and shifts to send shivers of glee and fear up my spine, even though I knew that the ice underfoot was over a foot

powerful, as anyone who has failed to pour antifreeze into a car radiator and suffered a cracked engine block knows. Ice can split rocks and bulldoze large humps of dirt onto the shoreline. When two expanding ice sheets press together in the middle of a lake, "ice heaves" or "pressure ridges" pile

thick and perfectly safe.

With the coming of spring and the higher and more intense rays of the sun, the ice begins to "rot." The melting first takes place along the junctures between the candles. The result is what's called "honeycomb" or "rotted ice." It looks very much like what I used to imagine as a crys-

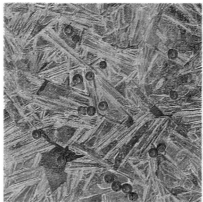

Whether it forms featherlike crystals on a windowpane or column-shaped ones over a puddle, water will only freeze at 32 degrees if it has a nucleus of dust or some other material around which to form. Pure water will not freeze until it reaches minus 40 degrees.

talline city of towers and turrets and passageways.

However you want to imagine this type of ice, stay off it. Even a thick sheet of honeycomb supports very little weight (see Chapter 13 on ice safety).

Spring's sun and warmer winds gnaw away until the ice breaks up into floes, and ultimately disappears completely. Sometimes a warm wind will blow the sheet of rotten ice to one shore of the lake, where it will accumulate in mounds of broken fragments. They may linger for several days or a few hours, tenaciously hanging on for a time but ultimately succumbing to the warmth of the fresh season, a rapidly shrinking testimonial to the winter that was.

SNOW, ICE, AND YOU

All winter outdoor activities depend on two properties. First, snow and ice are slippery. This allows you to move over them, often at a brisk clip.

Second, snow is sticky. This allows you to make things from it.

DID YOU KNOW

The careful observer of winter phenomena will notice what appear to be blobs of ice fastened to the bottom of a cold, swift-moving stream. The water often hovers at 32 degrees and is full of drifting disks called "frazil ice." When these strike rocks, they may stick and accumulate into blobs of "anchor ice." A big enough chunk of anchor ice can float the rock up off the bottom and carry it away downstream.

Water is one of the few liquids that expands when it turns to a solid — ice — rather than contracting. If it did not, ice skating would not exist, because ice would sink and form on the bottom of ponds and lakes.

Why Snow and Ice Are Slippery

By one estimate, the friction of the bottom of a ski moving across snow at speed can generate as much heat as a 100-watt lightbulb. The result is snowmelt; at any given point, below that ski is a micro-layer of water, which lubricates the board and facilitates its glide. The same phenomenon, in different degrees, explains the ability of a sled rail, skate, or the soles of your boots to slip and slide.

But if the cold is extreme, the heat generated by a ski or sled runner isn't enough heat to melt the crystals. Instead, hardened by the frigid temperatures, the crystals gouge into the surface like bits of stone. Early Arctic explorers whose sleds were equipped with metal runners reported that, during deep cold snaps, they felt they were dragging their sleds over sand

instead of snow. The Inuits avoided this problem by urinating on their sled runners if the temperature was very cold, thereby coating the runners with a layer of ice and rendering them equally as hard as the sharp snow crystals, thus repelling that gouging action. For the same reason, the colder the snow, the harder the wax a cross-country skier uses.

The movement of a skate blade across ice, one of the most slippery surfaces known, is possibly also aided by rotation of the molecular bonds, causing the water molecules to act like roller bearings.

Why Snow Sticks

Snow sticks together in two ways: by the bonding action of its particles, or through the presence of meltwater.

When snow crystals sit over hours or days in the snowpack they grow "sinters." These join the crystals together into a firm mass, in contrast to the loose powdery fluff that usually falls as new snow. You can speed the process by disturbing or "packing" the snow. Simply shoveling loose fresh snow into a pile breaks off the stellate arms and brings the snow crystals together, hastening sinter formation. This is the theory behind piling loose snow into a mound and letting it sit before you hollow out a quinzhee (see page 144).

If you compress loose, fluffy snow between your hands, you not only break off the tiny arms, but force those snow crystals together under pressure, causing them to fuse immediately one to the next. *Voilà*: a snowball.

We've all learned that wet snow packs more readily into a snow fort or snowball. This occurs become it contains tiny tunnels, or capillaries, filled with meltwater. When you bring two lumps of snow together, you not only fuse the crystals, but the meltwater in the capillaries of one handful joins the meltwater in the capillaries of the other handful. Thus the lumps "stick."

A ski or sled runner "sticks" in wet snow when tiny bridges of water

NATURE'S FREEZER CHEST

We tend to overlook a property of snow and ice because it is so obvious: They're cold. One way this property has served humankind for millennia is in food preparation and preservation.

Northern natives discovered frozen food long before they encountered Europeans. Raw walrus meat set out the night before a hunting expedition provided calorie-rich provisions, and the freezing process kept the fat from rancidity.

In 1915 Clarence Birdseye, trekking in Labrador, observed this process, noting that game cuts which froze in the dry Arctic air cooked up fresh and moist. Eight years later, Birdseye duplicated the phenomenon under controlled conditions and founded an industry. As you pilot your grocery cart past aisle after aisle of vegetables, meats, pizzas, pocket sandwiches, and TV dinners, you might pause to note that they owe their availability to a frozen haunch of caribou that caught Birdseye's attention 80 years ago.

The history of frozen food is not without tragedy. Three centuries before Birdseye's inspiration, the philosopher Francis Bacon was struck with a similar notion. While passing a Highgate butchery, Bacon found himself wondering whether cold could retard putrefaction. He leaped from his carriage, bought a freshly slaughtered hen, and stuffed it with snow. The fowl's fate is unrecorded, but Bacon's experiment brought on a case of bronchitis, which led to his death on April 9, 1626.

jump from the capillaries and adhere to the bottom. Thus ski waxes for wet snow are "hydrophobic" — water-repelling — and a drop of water will bead up on their surface.

Fresh powder that sits briefly in weather just above the freezing point makes the best sticky snow for building snowmen and sculptures or for forming snowballs.

In our experience, the very stickiest snow — the kind that makes the worst skiing but the finest snowballs to peg against a tree or roll into a snow sculpture — occurs in fresh powder that sits briefly in weather just above the freezing point. This is because fresh powder is riddled with many fine capillaries (compared to the fewer, larger capillaries you find in older, grainier snow). The slightly-above-freezing weather provides just enough thaw to fill the capillaries, but not so much as to soak the snow-pack like a sponge.

OBSERVING THE NATURAL WORLD

The outdoors seems more sterile in winter. Deciduous trees are denuded of their greenery. Varmints have apparently gone who knows where. The skies are more often gray, the winds more often predatory.

But this barrenness is to a great extent illusory. Dormant plant life is going through an elaborate adaptive process, husbanding resources in anticipation of the annual growth spurt that will begin in spring. Many small mammals are as active as at any other time of the year, scurrying about after food and to maintain high body temperature; voles, shrews, and lemmings may be burrowing in the very snow beneath your cross-country skis. For both you and nature, the more varied weather is an opportunity and a challenge.

Observing the world of winter is a recreation in itself, and provides one of the best opportunities for interaction with, and education of, your children. It serves as a fine introduction to aspects of natural science, natural history, and ecology, and as a springboard to discussions of the positive practices we seek to follow as responsible citizens of the backcountry. Further, two activities provide the opportunity to take home souvenirs of your excursion, even as you leave their source undisturbed.

With a little luck, you'll find entire tableaux suggesting melodramas to play out in your imagination. You spot, for instance, tiny pawprints that abruptly end at a large, fan-like pattern in the snow. Piecing together the scene like some cold-weather Sherlock Holmes, you deduce that here is where a hawk swept out of the sky and scooped up a scurrying mouse, leaving behind his wingprints as he flapped away.

A world of activity is writ large and clear in the snow. Here a tracker takes a closer look at the odd "footprint" left by the playful river otter, which slides along the snow on its belly.

ANIMAL TRACKING

A bit of close attention to animal tracks will quickly disabuse you of the preconception of winter's quietude. You'll soon learn to detect more comings and goings than in a New York City subway station during rush hour.

With visualization, you will discover more wildlife in the woods in winter. In summer, when tracks are fewer, you must spot animals in the flesh to "see" them, but in winter they leave a more complete record of their doings in the snow that lasts for hours or days. We've found that animal tracking while we're out on snowshoes or cross-country skis is one of the most absorbing and thought-provoking activities of winter. In trying to interpret the tracks and discern what they were up to, you begin to think like an animal might think, and see the terrain, and winter itself, the way an animal does.

Track Identification

Matching a track to the species that left it is a rewarding exercise in itself. It's particularly valuable in demonstrating to both children and neophyte hiking companions the vast variety of wildlife that shares our winter world.

A field guide (see Sources & Resources) is your basic reference for matching the footprint to the animal, and snow is the medium that captures and preserves tracks most effectively. But the drawings in guide books illustrate the ideal patterns; in the field, you'll find partial, obscured, and hastily left tracks.

Begin your training in your own backyard. If it is unfenced, and you or your neighbors keep pets, many of the animals that pass through will be domestic cats and dogs. Note the size and configuration of canine tracks, and compare them to matching tracks made while you can actually observe whether your visitor was Butch the mastiff, Charlie the golden retriever, or Fifi the toy poodle.

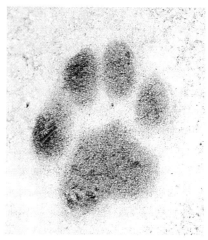

Top: Possum tracks along the shore of a frozen pond. Bottom: A bobcat track in central Massachusetts. The shy, nocturnal bobcat is seldom seen, making its vivid tracks that much more exciting to cross.

Look especially for unusual characteristics. Cats, because they are generally similar in size, are more difficult to distinguish one from the next. Still, when I step out on the deck in the morning after a fresh snowfall, I always know when Spike has been prowling about: He was born with the slight genetic defect of doubled forepaws, so his sign is unmistakable.

Without leaving your yard, extend your search to wild animals. With the help of your field guide, you should soon be able to identify small rodents, including squirrels, chipmunks, and field mice; non-migratory birds like magpies; and in the case where forage such as grass or last season's desiccated tomato plants rise above the snow, larger mammals like raccoons, rabbits, or deer. Bolster your identification by seeking out and learning to distinguish scat.

Now it's time to head into the field with trusty guidebook in hand. The best time of the day for tracking is early morning; in winter, most mammals are nocturnally active. A good spot to start is where two habitats meet, such as a forest's edge or a streambank.

Another aid to finding tracks is to observe other signs of recent animal activity in the general area, since most mammals tend to reduce their ranging distances in the cold to conserve calories. Lower tree

LIFE UNDER SNOW

At least a dozen species of small mammals, including some voles, mice, and shrews, become communal in winter, even though they lead solitary lives in the warmer seasons. Banding together, they make their homes beneath the snow.

This adaptation provides several advantages for survival. Taiga voles, for example, commonly form winter nests in groups of between five and ten individuals, huddling together to reduce overall body exposure. Their combined body heat can raise the ambient temperature of their burrow to as high as 25 degrees over the above-snow air temperature. Through an instinctive agreement, they emerge to find food only in subgroups, leaving the others behind to maintain the warmth of their snow caves.

The trade-offs of grouping include greater competition for available vittles, more chance of infection by disease or parasites, and a stronger scent that can attract natural enemies. But on balance, by working and playing nicely with others, these critters significantly increase their odds of seeing another spring.

branches that have been bitten recently or lack needles, as well as gnawed bark on the trunks, indicate the nearby presence of large herbivores such as deer, elk, or moose. Burrow holes provide ventilation for the subnivian nests of small mammals, and nearby you're likely to find the tracks they left on foraging missions.

At first, the tracks you find will fall into rough categories within which the differentiations are fundamental: claws, paws, hooves, horseshoe imprints, avian scratchings. But in time you'll begin to become a master sleuth of track identification. Essential clues include size, shape, toe configuration, and accompanying droppings.

A snowshoe hare dashed across an open stretch of snow toward a dense stand of trees. The hare's distinctive tracks are numerous and easy to spot, though few people can claim to have seen the animal itself.

What makes the detective game more fun is that tracks in snow often attempt to bamboozle you. Drifting, melting, and settling may partially obscure prints, or make them either larger or smaller than when they were originally left. If positive identification is impossible, try following the

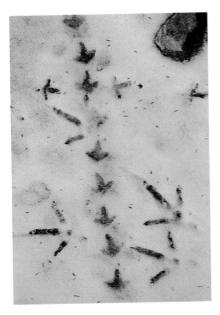

marks until you reach more shaded or sheltered terrain, where they may well become sharper and clearer.

Note also that tracks can be distorted, or even "formed," from above. When flummoxed, look skyward for a branch, power line, or the eave of a house. You might have been momentarily fooled by snow or ice melt that dribbled down to form an indentation that only looks like a footprint.

Accurately visualizing an animal that left a set of tracks is deeply satisfying. No matter where you live in snow country, you should be able, over time, to compile a life list of at least 100 critters. But as you do so, expand your pursuit to an examination of what the animal was doing when it left these marks.

Interpretation of Tracks

Close scrutiny of prints can reveal flight from a predator, stalking for food, or even snow sport not unlike your own recreation.

You pick up the trail of a deer. The prints are fairly closely spaced, and then become numerous and random under a conifer. Needles on the lower branches are missing; here the deer fed. Under the tree's shelter is a bowl-like depression formed by the deer's rolling, and nearby, a deeper pit, melted down by body heat during the animal's post-dinner nap. The tracks leading away are more widely spaced, indicating that the deer was awakened by the noise of humans or the

Top: Ruffed grouse and wild turkey tracks cross one another. Bottom: River otter tracks with typical tail drag showing on the snow.

approach of a hungry enemy, and sprinted for safety.

Coyote prints are set 5 inches apart, indicating careful stalking — and then the pawprints are three times as distant, leading to a ragged hole in the snow. Here the canine "dove" into the white stuff to seek a meal of some prey. The victim's tracks take off in wide lopes that veer from side to side, as it managed to escape temporarily. It turns this way and that; banked sloughs behind it denote that the larger animal was more clumsy and lost its footing in the course of the chase. Another depression is faintly stained with blood and bits of fur: For the wily coyote, dinner is served.

Small-mammal tracks may suddenly and mysteriously dead-end in the middle of nowhere. Keep looking. Some hares can leap as far as 5 feet, which likely means they were bounding frantically away from a pursuer. Tree squirrels might launch themselves at their target trunk from a range of 40 inches. If the tree is snow-plastered, look for marks of the ensuing climb.

BRINGING WINTER TRACKS HOME

Committed snow trackers might want to augment their life list of tracks by casting them in plaster of Paris, available in hobbyist shops. In the field, carry the powder in a double Ziploc-type bag, and have water available to make a mixture when you come upon a footprint that is pristine enough to warrant addition to your collection.

Unfortunately, a mark or sign made in snow will melt and deform when liquid is poured into it. Here's a way to deal with that problem; credit for its invention goes to E. Laurence Palmer, a naturalist at Cornell University in the 1950s.

This method works best in temperatures at zero or below. Add to your kit a small atomizer such as a plant sprayer, with the nozzle adjusted to a fine mist. When you encounter a print you wish to preserve, add snow to the water in the spritzer to bring it close to freezing, and apply a thin, even coat to the floor and sides of the track. Some tracking enthusiasts also like to ring the print with a collar of cardboard a few inches high; or you may prefer to just spray the snow around the print.

While the ice solidifies, mix up the plaster, again adding snow to chill it. Pour carefully into the ice-shelled depression, allow to set, and you'll have another trophy for your collection.

Look for tracks, like these of the river otter, where animals tend to congregate: along streams and on lakes and at the margins between fields and woods. Tracks stand out even more clearly early in the morning and in the afternoon when raking sunlight creates vivid shadows.

Animal signs can reveal pure playfulness. Should you discover numerous shallow rounded troughs cut vertically into the hardpack snow of a high-country slope in the spring, search at the bottom for pawprints 8 to 16 inches long, with five distinct toes. Black bear and grizzly bear cubs have often been observed "sledding," climbing back up for numerous rides, while the sow (who left the big prints at the foot of the hill) waits as patiently as any mother until the little ones tire of their fun. Similarly, the four-toed tracks of snowshoe hares might appear in an apparently aimless jumble spread over a wide circle. You've discovered a bunny hop: Like some slightly-odd humans we know, snowshoe hares sometimes dance in the snow for the sheer joy of it.

It is permissible to apply a latitude to your interpretation of the behaviors indicated by tracks, as long as it is based on sound biology. For children, these interpretations can challenge them and provoke further thoughtfulness.

Tracker's Alert

A few seasons back, we were hiking on hardpack late-spring snow in the high country when three things happened almost simultaneously. A companion said, "What's that smell?"; a rustle came from the thicket to our left; and a terrifying growl came from the hillside to our right.

We turned slowly in the latter direction to see a black bear sow erect on her haunches, her teeth bared. That told us what was in the thicket: We had inadvertently placed ourselves directly between the sow and her new cub.

The bear feinted a charge. We fought the urge to panic — and believe us, that was no easy mindfeat — and backed slowly away. When we'd made about 30 feet, the cub ambled out of the bushes, and mother and child, reunited, wandered back into the forest.

We were lucky. Large animals such as black bears, grizzly bears, moose, and mountain cats that are

WEATHER WATCH

Winter weather has a paradoxical reputation for being inexorable, yet capriciously changeable at the same time. We dwell on those cold snaps that seem as if they will never lift, or snowfall that goes on for days; yet we also associate winter with the blizzard that descends without warning and ceases as abruptly or, conversely, a sudden shift in a more benign direction, such as a rise in temperature. While observing these phenomena at their most extreme during one of your backcountry rambles is at best a once-in-a-lifetime experience, you might just be lucky enough to find yourself in the right place at the right time — like Louis Williams.

Williams, a resident of Spearfish, South Dakota, remembers the morning of January 22, 1943, as if it were yesterday. At 7:30, the temperature was minus 4 degrees. At 7:32, Dakotans were basking at 45 above. The rise of 49 degrees in 120 seconds is the most dramatic ever recorded on the planet, and a demonstration of the power of the chinook.

Called by climatologists a katabatic wind, chinooks are peculiar to the northwestern quarter of the country. They occur when warm Pacific air masses sweep east over the Northern Rockies or a subrange where the stabilizing moisture condenses, then shoot down to the flatland and elbow the cold aside like a rude passenger in a crowded elevator.

"What I remember isn't the warmth so much as the trees," Williams told us. "The timber south and east of town died before our eyes." Sensing premature spring, the trees let down their defenses, and perished within hours when the temperature fell once more.

Coincidentally, the continental-U.S. record for adamantly unchanging winter weather is held by the same region. On November 30, 1935, the temperature at Langdon, North Dakota, dropped below the freezing mark — and remained under it for the next 92 days. For 41 consecutive days toward the end of that period, the temperature refused to rise above zero.

rarely aggressive toward humans under normal circumstances can become fiercely protective when they believe their young are threatened. No matter how alert and careful you are, these confrontations do occur, though very rarely. If you find yourself in this situation, slowly raise your arms to make yourself "bigger" and thus a more formidable enemy, maintain eye contact, and move away quietly and slowly.

Most importantly, *do not run.* Animal behaviorists argue the reasons for bears' reaction to headlong flight, but do not question the empirical evidence: Bears perceive slow retreat as concessionary, but a mad dash as provocative.

Statistically, you are more threatened by other humans. Although the vast majority of hunters are careful and conscientious, during the season we try to keep our forays to off-limits areas. If you do venture into hunting grounds, wear a bright "hunter-orange" overvest; in some regions, it may be required by law.

Equally important, remember that you can be a threat to the animals. Big game such as elk suffered from winter kill long before humans were present, but our invasion into their habitat by way of the expansion of suburbia and increased interest in winter recreation has stressed them further during the cold months. Elk, deer, and moose walk a tightrope between sufficient food intake and caloric expenditure, and you should not upset this balance by your presence. When tracking these animals, abandon your pursuit well before you actually get within scenting distance. High-speed flight at the sight or smell of you can cause fatal exhaustion.

Finally, if you live on the edge of a game range, the urge to set out feed is seductive; we've experienced it ourselves after observing on winter hikes elk whose rib cages showed beneath their hides. Fight that urge; remember that wild animals are not pets. If you provide food for them, they become habituated, and may lose the will to forage. Your kindness, no matter how well meant, harms big game in the long run. In a recent April, for example, forty elk carcasses were found on the outskirts of West Yellowstone, Montana — all within 100 yards of a field where residents provided hay for them during the winter.

I C E   S K A T I N G

A New England friend of ours recently took his family on a skating expedition that resembled the hard-water version of a canoe trip. They parked a car several miles downstream along a sluggish frozen river, packed a picnic lunch, and parents and children skated away downstream over the glassy surface. They explored the shoreline coves and beaver dams, studied the river bottom through the clear ice, and built a warm fire on the frozen surface when they stopped for lunch.

"That was a real winter adventure," he told us later. "So much of the skating today is done indoors on artificial rinks that you forget the sense of freedom and adventure of real ice."

This is exactly how we feel about ice skating. We love to play hockey, indoors or out, and appreciate the beauty of figure skating and ice dancing on an arena, but for us the truest form of skating is simply to glide out on a frozen pond or river. We're set free from the constraints of the everyday world and, like some sort of ice bird, glide onward, skate stroke after skate stroke, forever.

As children, we loved to peer down through the ice and study the weedbeds, logs, and sunken rowboats lying on the silent lake bottom. The ice itself fascinated us with its myriad patterns of air bubbles, resembling the

hockey. In this gentle but vigorous game, skating skill and stick handling were minor factors. The slower skaters played goalie or defense and the rest of the crew chased the puck in a knot of bodies flailing across the ice like some winter tornado.

WHERE TO FIND NATURAL ICE

You can come by natural ice more easily than you might think. It forms on lakes and ponds for at least part of the

While some of the best natural ice conditions lie farther to the south, this lake in the Canadian Rockies, covered by only a dusting of snow, offers excellent ice skating.

crystal cities of a lost world. We'd join hands and play crack the whip. Ultimately the person on the end broke loose and careened off across the ice as if launched into orbit, while my mother elegantly practiced figure-eights.

Weekends, when dads were around, family members of all ages and both genders got together on the frozen lake for games of pickup

winter in much of the United States, the Deep South excepted. The best, however, lies in the ice belt, a band a few hundred miles wide that sits just north of the 40th parallel. This region receives plenty of cold but is far enough south to escape deep snows, which make skating difficult without a lot of shoveling.

Residents of southern New England, New York, New Jersey, and midwestern regions like Michigan, Wisconsin, and southern Minnesota have some of the best ice in the world at their disposal. These states claim long traditions of ice sports, from speed skating to iceboating to simple skating. People who live closer to the North Pole still find abundant ice, if they don't mind clearing it of snow, while those who live farther south can make their own rinks during a cold snap (see page 112).

Newly formed ice, like this black ice on Five Bridges Pond in Califronia's Owens Valley, will support several people standing together when it is four inches thick.

It's possible to find natural ice in the mountain states of the West, although elevation presents the same problems, as well as opportunities, as latitude. Too high in the mountains and the snows bury the ice; too low and the winter doesn't freeze hard enough to maintain a solid ice sheet. Reservoirs behind dams often do the trick, but avoid moving water. Due to the terrain, most western rivers flow too fast to form decent ice.

What to Watch Out For

Not unreasonably, many people who are new to natural ice fear it and question its ability to support them. But with common sense and caution, you'll come to feel comfortable on these glistening, gem-like surfaces.

Lakes and ponds generally make the best skating surfaces. Skaters must use more caution on rivers because the current can cause weak spots in an otherwise solid surface. Rivers also pose the additional danger that, if you fall through, the flow may pull you under the ice. In any case, rivers must be *slow moving* even to consider them for skating, securely frozen, and, like all ice, cautiously checked before you venture out.

For a general rule of thumb for natural, newly formed ice, 4 inches of thickness is usually safe for several people to stand together (not on which to drive a car, however). It helps to carry an axe, pry bar, or other object

Lakes do not always freeze uniformly. Protected, shallow bays like this one on Lake Champlain may provide excellent skating long before open water freezes over.

much less weight per inch than more elastic new ice.

For more on safety on ice, and rescue techniques, see Chapter 13.

HOW TO CHOOSE A PAIR OF ICE SKATES

There came a time in my youth when I hated skating. I knew how to skate, and used to *love* to skate, but every time I skated I painfully froze my toes.

Finally I acquired a pair that fit and my toes miracu-

with which to break through the ice to check its thickness.

Note that lakes do not always freeze uniformly. New ice especially may freeze more thinly in some areas, notably near springs in a lake bottom or eddies in a river. Likewise, the rotten ice of springtime — what's known as "honeycomb" ice because of its perforated character — supports

lously thawed. No longer were they crammed in the front of the skate boot like mushrooms in a packing case, the circulation cut off. Suddenly I rediscovered skating's pleasure.

Ill-fitting skates probably rank as the single greatest cause of problems experienced by beginning skaters. The temptation is great to buy a pair of skates too large for a child and let her "grow into them," or to make do with a pair of too small hand-me-downs.

A skate that is too tight will cause painful pinches, and constrictive footwear of any kind that is poorly insulated also promotes frozen toes. Conversely, an over-large skate provides little ankle support. This often leads to a parent's diagnosis of "weak ankles." Skating coaches say there is virtually no such thing, and that with correctly fitted skates ankles miraculously strengthen.

One choice that you'll have to make from the start is whether to buy figure skates or hockey skates. Probably the most fundamental difference is that a figure skate's bowed blade allows the skater to spin easily on the axis, and to skate backward or forward. A hockey skate's straight blade

helps it grip the ice to push off into a sprint start or when making high-speed turns. In other words, a figure skate is more maneuverable, a hockey skate more stable at high speed and in quick stops. You can play pickup hockey on figure skates but you will not skate with the same stability as a player wearing hockey skates.

Some sporting-goods stores carry skates only as a sideline and don't employ salespeople who are qualified to help you choose the best model for you. Consult a hockey or skating coach in your area and ask where to find the best selection of skates and most expert staff. Often this will be a skate shop that's attached to or located near a skating rink.

Expect to pay from

(Left) A figure skate's bowed blade provides greater maneuverability while (right) a hockey skate's straight blade helps it grip the ice for quick starts and high speed truns.

Quality skates are expensive, but worth every penny in comfort and performance. Skate swaps are the best way to outfit children with quality, reasonably priced gear.

$65 to $300 for a new pair of adult hockey skates, and from $100 to $200 for recreational figure skates (competition skates cost considerably more). Children's hockey skates run from $40 to $180, and a decent pair of beginner's figure skates for children begins at about $60. If you can afford them, both children and adults will learn much more quickly on higher quality, more expensive skates than on flimsier, cheaper models.

If you live in an area where skating or hockey is particularly popular, you might be able to find an annual "skate swap," where you'll find many pairs of skates brought in by parents whose children have outgrown them and who are looking for a larger pair. Some skate shops also

offer a "trade-in" program on used skates, and sell used as well as new skates, for much less. If you do buy a used pair of skates, make sure that the toe box is not frayed, and that the boot retains support around the ankle and hasn't become floppy.

Your choice depends on the type of skating you wish to pursue. Some coaches suggest that because the boot of the figure skate is closer to the ice, it provides more inherent ankle support and is an easier skate to master. Racing skates, similar to hockey skates but with a lower boot and long blade that extends several inches past the boot's heel and toe, are specialized gear and generally should be avoided by beginners.

Double-runner skates for children — those with two blades mounted side by side — are counter-productive as a learning device. They'll allow a toddler to walk on ice, but don't expect to teach anyone who is wearing them to skate.

Correct Fitting

When skating you'll wear a relatively thin sock of silk, polypropylene, or a similar material. Thick wool socks reduce ankle support and cramp your toes, making them colder rather than warmer. In trying on a pair of skates, wear the sock you'll don on the ice.

The skate should fit snugly; depending on the manufacturer, the right skate for you might be a full size smaller than your street shoe. You should be able to wiggle your toes, but your heels should not slip when you walk around in them.

Properly lacing your skates is an art in itself, and sometimes, when our fingers are cold and we're in a hurry to get on the ice, one we feel we haven't quite mastered after all these years. Kick back your heel and begin to lace tightly. After you've tightened a short distance up the boot, kick your heel again, and continue to tighten.

Skate Maintenance

A properly sharpened blade is key to effective skating. Your blades should be free of nicks and burrs, sharpened at the beginning of each winter, and sharpened during the season as well if they start to feel dull. This will depend on the type of ice you skate

on, how dirty it is, and how many hours you've skated. A hockey- or figure-skate blade is what's known as "hollow ground" — it resembles two knife edges lying side by side with a "hollow" carved into the steel between them, like a ditch or drain-pipe. As with an alpine ski, when you turn, you use one edge or the other to grip the ice.

Many sporting-goods stores have the equipment to sharpen skates, but the skate shop of a rink generally does the best job. Occasionally a skate-sharpener will inadvertently hone your blades so one edge is higher than the other, which gives you an uneven grip. To check for equal blade height, turn your skate upside down, lay a quarter on the bottom of your blade, and sight down the blade as if it were a rifle barrel. The quarter should rest flat at each point along the length of the blade.

FIVE TIPS FOR BETTER SKATING

Advanced hockey and figure skating demand different styles and tech-niques, but fundamental principles apply to both.

❶ Beginning skaters often make the mistake of trying to propel them-selves forward by pushing off with their toe, as if walking. A skater always gets her forward thrust by pushing to the side. Figure skaters don't use the sharp teeth on the front of their skates — called "picks" —

The "picks" on the toes of figure skate blades are used for making spins and jumps, not to provide forward momentum.

to the side with one foot at a time, as you would when skating forward. Push with your right skate so your blade inscribes almost a crescent shape on the ice, transfer your weight and glide for a moment on your left skate, then push with the left, and glide on the right.

④ When making a crossover

to propel themselves forward. They are there for use in maneuvers like spins and jumps.

② The key to making an abrupt stop is to twist your shoulders opposite to the direction in which you turn your skates. You begin a stop to the left, for instance, by turning both your upper body and your skates toward the left. As your skates begin to skid to the left, twist your shoulders back to the right. This helps your blades dig into the ice and prevents your body from simply spinning in a leftward direction.

③ Many beginners try to skate backward by waggling their feet in unison. Bend your knees and push off

during a turn (the action of stepping one skate inside the other), make sure to bend the knee of the skate that's on the ice. The skate stroke you make to the outside should be a quick thrust.

⑤ Don't worry about falling on the ice — not that it won't happen. If you don't take the occasional spill, you're probably not trying hard enough. The secret to avoiding injury is to *relax*. Watch a small child learning to walk: whenever they get into trouble and are about to topple, they'll buckle their knees and land harmlessly on their bottoms. Nor do you have to be a toddler to fall properly. Figure-skating champion

Maribel Vinson Owen reports how her mother skated twice weekly at the age of seventy-nine and fell almost every time, but was never hurt because she knew how to relax like a tumbler.

PICKUP HOCKEY

The old joke "I went to a fight, and a hockey game broke out" does not apply to the hockey we play. That is not to say we are dainty; these contests involve as intense a workout as you could ask

Plenty of novice skaters are threatened by the roughness of hockey. But friendly pickup games including men, women, and sometimes children, while vigorous, are purely pleasurable.

for, and every day as we sit at our keyboards we look forward with pleasurable anticipation to four in the afternoon five days a week, and nine in the morning on Saturdays and Sundays. It is then that the games begin.

The action is aggressive and genteel at the same time; one member of our group played well into her pregnancy. Our crew is a motley collection of schoolteachers, bricklayers, wheat ranchers, students, writers, a

Racing skates resemble hockey skates, but have low cut boots and longer blades that extend well beyond the boot's toe and heel.

lawyer or two (you have to watch out for them), plus the aforementioned mother, who in the summer guides wilderness expeditions on llamas.

The rules are essentially the same as regular hockey, with a more casual interpretation. Checking is forbidden; you can't intentionally run into someone as is allowed in college and NHL hockey. Tempers are checked at the door; flare-ups are no more vigorous than you'd find in your average game of soccer.

The play is still fast and furious, however. Our rink is small enough that we have no blue lines and call offsides only in the most flagrant cases, more or less guessing where the blue line should be. The skaters on the rink across town judge the blue lines according to the location of two streetlight poles.

For equipment, players generally wear a slightly lighter version of regulation gear: hockey skates, shin and knee pads, elbow pads, helmets, mouthguards, and (for the males) cups. Some wear sweatpants, while others prefer hockey britches with their built-in hip, thigh, and tailbone pads.

The other major difference in our

In pickup hockey tempers are checked at the door and checking — intentionally running into an opponent — is strictly forbidden.

version is that players are not allowed to lift or shoot the puck off the ice. This makes scoring a special challenge. For the "cage" we use a single 5-foot length (the standard width of a goal is 6 feet) of two-by-four laid on the ice, which is plenty hard to hit when guarded by a defender and provides an incentive to observe the "no-lifting" rule. When we have enough players we rotate a defender back to the cage to play goalie. Instead of seeing the red light and hearing the buzzer when you score, the plank makes the most satisfying *thunk*! That's when your teammate will raise his or her stick jubilantly into the air and shout "Lumber!"

During our weekday games, we cordon off one end of the rink, about a third of its total area, so the neighborhood children have a place to skate after school. We've found that the ideal number of players for the size of our weekday, shortened rink is four or five per team; more than that and the ice becomes too crowded and the playing confused. If more of our regular players show up than we have room for, we usually rotate one or two players off the ice, each person taking their turn to sit out of the game for a few minutes.

We have no set teams and usu-ally rely on one of our number, Lu Haas, a teacher who is used to orga-nizing unruly bunches, to divide us into two more or less equally weighted teams. The game usually lasts until it's too dark to see the puck — which generally means about 5:30. The grueling, 2-hour games on Sat-

A RINK OF YOUR OWN

Where we grew up in the ice belt, nature took care of rink construc-tion by way of the many lakes, but in the Northern Rockies where we now live, most water is relatively narrow and swift moving. To indulge our passion for hockey, the rink building is up to us.

Each December finds us spending several frosty mid-nights in a local park flooding a shallow depression in the earth with a firehose. We come home with cold toes and fingers, looking like wooly mammoths encrusted in layers of ice. The payoff is the promise of vigorous pickup games at the end of each workday, and longer contests on weekend mornings. Outside our reserved time, the neighborhood kids enjoy skating and sliding on the ice we make.

Here's the ice-making method that our local guru, English pro-fessor and former semi-pro goalie Bill Bevis, has perfected over the years through trial and error:

Ideally, you'll want some snow cover and the forecast of a cold snap. Choose a flat spot in your yard or park where there is a slight depression in the ground. (Years ago, a bulldozer sculpted a low spot in the park to form a suitable location for our rink.) Using shovels or a riding lawn-mower, pack the snow firmly; this white underlayer pays dividends late in the season, reflecting the spring sun's melting rays to pre-serve the ice.

Spray a light layer of water with a hose to coat the snow with a thin glaze of ice, then place a lawn sprinkler on the rink to lay down the initial base of ice. Bevis rec-ommends a rotary sprinkler of the kind with an arm that periodically whacks against the jet of water; this jerking motion helps knock off the ice that will form on the sprinkler head. An outdoor tem-

urday and Sunday mornings bring out our full roster of players — about fifteen — but we use the full length of the rink, so we can accommodate teams of six players. We belong to no league, but several times each winter we revive our good-natured rivalry with the group across town. We'll square off on a Sunday morning on their full-sized rink, as a few sleepy fans sip coffee in the stands.

BROOM BALL

Broom ball is low-tech hockey — of an antic variety — for those who

---

perature of between 10 degrees and 28 degrees works best; below 10 degrees the sprinkler won't function effectively. The sprinkler also must be checked once an hour and excess ice knocked off with a screwdriver. It helps to apply some WD-40 or anti-freeze to the sprinkler before you start.

You must move the sprinkler periodically to build an even coat of ice. In 36 hours, we can apply about 3 inches of ice to our rink with a sprinkler operating on the high water pressure from our industrial well and pump; it would probably take longer using a home water system. Once you've laid down a couple of inches of ice with the sprinkler, use a garden or fire hose (our pump takes the latter) and spray the rink with coats of ice to finish evening the surface. You'll need a total ice thickness of at least 2 inches before you can skate without breaking through the surface.

The ice will need periodic resurfacings after it's chewed up by blades. The secret to this, says Bill, is to coat the rink with *thin layers*. Too much water at one time causes the top to chip and crack, or to freeze on the surface and allow the water underneath to form air pockets.

Our "boards" around the rink are nothing more than the snowbanks that accumulate on the rink's perimeter during the season's shoveling, although we sometimes sculpt these into low walls and spray them to form an ice coat.

Ours is quite large for a homemade rink — about 120 x 60 feet (a regulation National Hockey League rink measures 200 x 85 feet). An alternate method to building a rink, especially a smaller rink, is to make an enclosure out of low boards. Some rink builders favor 2-foot-high lengths of plywood staked into the earth.

Broom ball is an antic variety of hockey devised by those who would rather not skate. It makes for a hilarious good time.

would rather not skate. Indeed, the regulation footwear is rubber galoshes of the zip-up-the-front variety. These provide just enough grip for clumsy locomotion, and enough slip for frequent and amusing spills.

The venue is any expanse of ice large enough to accommodate the number of players, which can range from two on a side to mob rule. Each player is equipped with a straight-blade broom; the "puck" is a basketball, volleyball, or soccer ball. At either end of the ice is the goal: It may be a jerry-built frame of two-by-fours; a soccer cage, or even a couple of tipped-over park benches. You'll want it about 10 feet wide.

The goaltenders are the only players allowed to use their hands, although goalies may employ their brooms as well, and they can also fling the ball down the ice after saving it. No checking is allowed; the ball, not other players, is the broom's object.

Otherwise, the rules are freestyle: After each goal, a member of the non-scoring team puts the ball in play by tossing it between the faced-off captains, and it is every person for himself. As with any respectable sport, trickery is allowed: Head fakes, feigned passes, and elusive dribbles are permissible and admired.

ICEBOATING

9

We once heard a first-time passenger compare iceboating to sitting in one of those fighter rocketships that zips in formation through tunnel-like matrices in the *Star Wars* movies. It's an apt metaphor for the sensation of what the surface of a frozen lake looks like rushing at you a few inches beneath the cockpit at 60 or 80 or even 100 miles per hour — no problem for an iceboat — as other crafts join you in a tight echelon or peel off into sharp turns. If you enjoy speed, you'll find few more exhilarating experiences in life — as iceboaters are forever pointing out — than a high-velocity ride across a frozen lake.

The magic derives from the nearly frictionless glide of a steel runner on ice propelled by a stiff breeze blowing against an airfoil-shaped sail. Iceboaters will tell you that their boats "generate their own wind." A puff of wind pushes the iceboat forward, and that initial forward motion forces more air to wash over the airfoil-like sail. Following the same laws of aerodynamics that keep an airplane wing aloft, that flow of air over the sail's curved surface drives the boat forward faster still.

Because of this phenomenon, iceboats are capable of sailing much faster than the velocity of the wind; with a moderate 15-mile-an-hour breeze you can scream along at four or five times that speed. *The Guinness Book of Records* lists the iceboating record at 143 miles an hour, clocked in 1938 at Lake Winnebago, Wisconsin.

The Dutch invented the first modern iceboats, although there's some evidence that Scandinavians sailed on ice as early as 2000 B.C. By the eighteenth century, the Dutch were rigging runners on the hulls of small sloops and sailing them over the frozen canals. The sport came to this country in 1790 when Oliver Booth built an iceboat in Poughkeepsie, New York, and sailed it on the frozen Hudson River.

The Hudson was a major center of iceboating by the late 1800s and wealthy New Yorkers raced each other in great "ice yachts," such as John E. Roosevelt's 48-foot-long *Icicle*. In the era before the automobile, iceboats ranked as the fastest vehicles on earth; a February 1871 drawing in *Frank Leslie's Illustrated Newspaper* shows the *Icicle* and a competitor named the *Zephyr* outracing the Chicago-New York express train, as it highballed along the shores of the Hudson. In 1885 the *Scud* hit a speed of 107 miles per hour.

ICEBOATING OPPORTUNITIES

Iceboating requires large expanses of snow-free ice, which occur only in certain regions. Far in the north, you can find plenty of frozen lakes, but the snow falls so deeply that it buries the ice; far to the south, the winter doesn't remain cold enough for the lakes to stay frozen for long.

The sport flourishes in that narrow band of the country known as the ice belt. This belt runs roughly above the 40th parallel from the East Coast to the Plains, and in Europe roughly along the 50th parallel. Even here, however, ice conditions change dramatically at nature's whim. Some years, iceboaters sail over great ice all winter long; other years, a heavy, wet snow might fall a few hours after a lake freezes, ruining it for the rest of the season.

The motto of iceboaters is *carpe diem* — seize the day. The moment good ice appears anywhere within a hundred miles, dedicated iceboaters will load their gear and set off, knowing that the perfect conditions could disappear under snow the next day. In some areas, iceboaters set up hotline networks to share reports of ice conditions.

When we lived in the ice belt, we tried to copper our bets in planning for winter sport: If it snowed, we went cross-country or downhill skiing or sledding, and if it didn't, we went iceboating. This is one attraction for skiers and snow sport enthusiasts — if you don't have snow, you needn't be frustrated, because you'll almost always have great ice instead.

Iceboating today is a small and esoteric sport but one whose partici-

The thrill of iceboating derives from the nearly frictionless glide of steel runners on ice, regularly propelling the vessels at 80 or even 100 miles an hour.

pants are passionate, even obsessed. You can find iceboats scattered here and there throughout much of the East and Midwest but the activity flourishes in a few pockets: in upstate New York and near Detroit, Milwaukee, and Minneapolis. While we've never heard of any iceboating "schools" or outfitters, the members of clubs are generally willing to introduce you to the sport.

For some reason, iceboating hasn't caught on much in the Plains, where we'd think you could find plenty of ice and certainly no lack of wind. Nor do you see much iceboating in the West, where we live now. The mountain snows generally ruin the good ice, although some low-elevation lakes seem to remain fairly clear. But there simply isn't much of a tradition of ice sports in the West; instead people look up to the mountains and that abundant snow. We're hoping that someday that will change and they'll look to lower elevations and those frozen lakes.

Types of Iceboats

Early Dutch iceboats consisted of a small sailboat with an outrigger-like plank mounted under the mast. A runner was mounted on each end of this plank, and the boat was steered by means of a third, movable runner fixed to the rudder at the rear of the boat, so the boat rode on three points.

This Dutch prototype became more or less the standard design of iceboats until early in the twentieth century. Known as a "stern steerer," the design functioned well except for one major flaw — a heavy puff of wind from aft tended to lift the rudder off the ice and send the boat into a wild, uncontrollable spin. Veteran iceboaters who used this old model learned to watch carefully for that rudder to start to twitch, or "flicker," as it was about to lift.

About 1930, the first "front-steering" iceboats made their appearance in the United States as a response to the flicker problem. This is the standard design of most of today's iceboats. Taking the Dutch prototype and spinning it around backward, the "runner plank" is mounted near the rear of the boat and the steering runner is mounted far to the front. Another innovation was to sleeken the "boat" to a skeletal framework. Viewed from above, it resembles a **T**, with the pilot sitting in a cockpit at the rear.

Some of the more famous designs over the years were the big stern-steering "A" and "B" boats that carried several passengers; the long, sleek, lightning-fast "Skeeter"; and the sporty little "DN." This latter was the winner of a design contest sponsored in the 1930s by the *Detroit News*, whose initials now are displayed on hundreds of iceboat sails throughout the country.

The DN is by far the most popular class of iceboat, and there are about 1,000 members in the DN association in North America and an equal number in Europe. Among the boat's appeal are its simplicity, portability (it weighs 125 pounds, measures 12 feet, and can be dismantled for transport), and relatively low cost, about $1,800 retail, with kits or plans available for less.

The DN has room for only one person in its open cockpit. A popular two-person boat with an enclosed cockpit is the Nite, measuring 18 feet and combining a little of everything — portability, speed, and roominess. The designer and manufacturer, Dick Slates of S & R Marine in Pewaukee, Wisconsin, reports that he's even received orders from the Saudis, who mount wheels on the boats and race them on the hot desert sands. Slates attends an annual "land-yachting" regatta in Nevada, another use to which you can put your iceboat.

Originally designed as a rescue craft on Long Island's Great South Bay, the Scooter is a hybrid iceboat and sailboat. It resembles a small sailboat with runners mounted against the hull rather than out on a runner plank. It's sailed with one side of the hull off the ice like a heeling sailboat. The traditional model has the handy capability to sail off the ice, over a patch of open water, and back onto the ice again, although today's racing Scooters are better limited to jumping small potholes.

How to Sail an Iceboat

Iceboating technique is not difficult to learn and in some ways is easier

The sporty "DN" iceboat is by far the most popular, with hundreds of the portable single-person craft in use all across the country.

than sailing on water. The rigging, sails, and general hardware of an iceboat are simpler than most racing boats. Likewise, a "soft-water sailor" must carefully haul in or let out the sail to precisely catch the wind for the boat to move efficiently; a "hard-water sailor," due to the enormous speed and airfoil effect of the sail, keeps his sail close-hauled much of the time — so tightly that the sail, as Slates puts it, resembles "a piece of plywood."

Practically speaking, this means that in a good breeze you can sail in different directions by making only minor adjustments. Some principles are the same as lake or ocean sailing: If the sail starts to flap, or luff, you've headed too far into the wind. You obtain maximum speed from an iceboat, like a sailboat, with the true wind coming at you directly from the side, or beam. Because the iceboat moves several times faster than the wind, however, the "apparent wind" will actually be coming at you almost from the bow. One trickier aspect of iceboating is to learn how to tell from what direction the "true wind" hits the sail.

Tacking upwind is relatively easy because the sail will luff if you head too close. But sailing across the wind or downwind becomes more difficult, leaving iceboat pilots to study the streaks of snow blowing across the ice and other signs of the true wind direction. Iceboat racers have been known to whip their craft into a 360-

Iceboat racers follow many of the same rules and tactics of their "soft-water" cousins, but they cover comparable distances in a third the time.

degree circle in the middle of a meet to test just which way the true wind blows.

Another odd aspect of iceboating occurs on a downwind leg. The soft-water sailor usually steers the boat straight downwind, but the hard-water boater finds it faster to zigzag or "tack" the boat to reach a destination that lies directly downwind. This is one reason for an old saying about piloting an iceboat. As Frederic M. Gardiner puts it in *Wings on the Ice*, "Anybody can sail an iceboat to windward, but you have to know your onions to bring her home."

Iceboats move fastest when one runner is barely lifting off the ice, like a sailboat at a slight heel. This makes for some of the most exciting iceboating — racing along balanced on two points and working the sail in and out to keep the boat balanced at the perfect angle as the wind screams in your face and the ice chips fly.

Sometimes a gust will suddenly tilt an iceboat up 30 degrees or more, and very occasionally an iceboat will tip over like a sailboat, with the difference, of course, that it's moving a lot faster and the "water" is a lot harder than the summertime version. A spill usually results in little damage to boat or pilot, although broken masts and bruises are a distinct possibility. Many pilots have gone for long skids along the ice surface and escaped unharmed.

The one nasty spill that I remember during my iceboating

years was when I had the bright idea of tying a sled to the back of my DN and pulling a friend along on it. The problem was that a strong gust hit at the moment when the sled happened to be twisted sideways. It acted like an anchor, preventing the iceboat from shooting forward fast enough to absorb the force of the puff. Instead, the boat flipped, pitching me out and crashing down on top of me. More worrisome than the bruised ribs was the prospect of explaining the broken mast to the old man, although, as I remember, he handled it well.

Iceboating Safety

The potentially high speeds and sometimes precarious nature of iceboating dictate certain precautions.

● Always wear a sturdy helmet — such as a motorcycle helmet — against the possibility of banging your head on the ice. Goggles protect your eyes from flying ice chips.

● It's a good idea to sail with another iceboat present, or at least with observers nearby, to monitor you for mishaps.

● Take extra care when approaching shorelines, as well as skaters, ice fishermen, other iceboats, and anyone

ICEBOAT RACING

With speed at the essence of the sport, it's inevitable that most serious iceboaters are also racers. An iceboat race is set up much like a sailboat race. The boats line up facing 45 degrees or so off the wind. At the starting gun, the pilots push their boats by running with them along the ice on boots fitted with metals spikes called creepers, hop aboard, and trim their sails.

A typical race consists of several laps over an upwind leg and a downwind leg of about a mile each, with recycled Christmas trees sometimes serving as windward and leeward "buoys." The boaters typically cover the entire three or four laps in an elapsed time of only fifteen minutes, compared to several times longer for a softwater race of similar length.

With the boats zipping among each other at high speeds, right-of-way rules are of paramount importance, and generally resemble those of sailboat racing. Tactics also resemble sailboat racing, with the difference that "covering" an opponent's sail with your own to foul his air plays an even greater role in iceboat racing. Because of their speeds, the stirred up air left in the wake of an iceboat can significantly slow the boat behind it.

else with whom you are sharing the ice. Iceboats lack brakes. You slow down or stop by heading into the wind and letting your sail flap, or luff, gradually gliding to a standstill. Making zigzag turns while heading into the wind helps to slow you, but you'll still need plenty of room to allow your craft to come to a halt.

⬤ Thoroughly test the ice conditions before you start sailing, and watch out particularly for cracks, pressure ridges, and patches of open water. The worst accident we know about occurred when an iceboat moving at high speed crashed into open water.

⬤ The wind chills aboard an iceboat can reach unspeakable lows. Ice-boaters generally favor snowmobile suits and insulated boots.

SKATE SAILING

I have not skate-sailed since my youth, though I am thinking of taking it up again. In preparation, I have already bought my bow tie.

My grandfather loved to skate-sail. I remember him winging across the ice with his racing skates going *clickety-clack* over the bumps and his flannel trouser legs projecting beneath the skate sail and flapping wildly in the winter wind. Always, an essential part of his costume was that bow tie — and not the clip-on type, mind you. Perhaps it was a talisman, but I think not. Grandfather simply refused to let his sartorial guard down when he left the parlor for the ice.

Bow tie or no, skate sailing is the minimalist among ice/wind sports.

FAR GONE WITH THE WIND

One of the latest — and wildest — snow and ice sports is what's called "kite skiing." You don a pair of regular alpine skis, take hold of a set of control lines that are connected to a paraglide-like kite or "foil," and are towed like a water-skier across a snow-covered lake or field at speeds up to 50 miles an hour. Like an iceboat, the device travels faster than the speed of the wind — two to four times faster — and an expert can jump off snowdrifts or cornices to heights of ten or more feet. "It's as if the water-skiing boat that's towing you is up in the air," says champion kite skier Steve Shapson.

Shapson says a beginner can learn the ropes in half an hour. A Finnish innovation called a skimbat, resembling a small hang glider that you hold near your body, also propels the skier over snowy surfaces and allows short airborne glides. (See Sources & Resources for more information on kite skiing.)

All you need is a pair of hockey or racing skates and a sail that resembles a 9-foot-long kite. This can range from a fancy store-bought model to the casual or even crude. We know one fellow who made a skate sail from bedsheets and the banisters of his apartment building's staircase.

Wear a sturdy helmet, such as a motorcycle helmet, and goggles when iceboating.

To sail, you balance the crosspieces of the airfoil over the shoulder on the upwind side of your body, turning yourself into a self-contained iceboat. Your body is the mast of an iceboat, your skates the runners. (Serious skate sailors use long-bladed racing skates, although hockey skates will do.) You trim by moving the sail forward and back across the shoulder, thus pivoting it to the wind, and steer with your skates. To come about to another tack, lift the sail over your head. In heavy air, a skate sailor actually leans over on his sail to brace it against the wind, and can reach speeds of 55 miles per hour.

ICE SURFING

Although it's been around for decades, skate sailing is not a well-known sport and the Skate Sailing Association of America counts only about 175 members (see Sources & Resources for its address). A similar ice-and-wind sport that's gained greater popularity in recent years goes by the name of "ice sailing" or, better to distinguish it from other ice sports, "ice surfing" or "ice boarding."

Increased interest in ice surfing parallels the windsurfing boom of the last 15 years or so. Summertime windsurfers who didn't want to hang

An ice surfer employs a standard windsurfing sail attached to...in this case a pair of alpine skis, although much improvisation marks this young sport.

trucks (these are available for about $50 from a skateboard or windsurf shop). Ice surfers wear padding on knees, elbows, and rear end or hips (hockey pads and pants will serve). The sport is easier to learn than windsurfing, ice surfers claim, because the waves don't jar you about, although one eleven-year-old Colorado windsurfer-turned-ice-surfer had another reason for liking it better.

"Ice surfing is safer," he told us. "I don't have to worry that something is going to swim up and get me."

up their sailboard rigs found a way to equip them with runners that are mounted on pivoting "trucks" like those of a skateboard. With these rigs, they would "surf" on the ice.

Essentially the technique is the same as windsurfing. You stand on the board and hold the sail from the upwind side, leaning your back to counterbalance the wind pressure against the sail. To turn, you move your weight on the board to make it pivot in the desired direction.

You can use a regular windsurfing sail rig, and buy a winter board and runners for about $500. These are available at windsurfing shops in northern regions of the country. Or you can make your own board out of plywood or fiberglass, machine a set of blades, and mount them on factory-made skateboard

ICE CLIMBING

W hen Jon Kienberger took me into western Montana's Bitterroot Mountains to introduce me to ice climbing, he told me the frozen waterfall we'd climb was about 30 degrees for the first section, and a "little steeper" after that. I envisioned a gentle staircase of ice leading to a small pillar.

Imagine my surprise when, after a 2-mile hike up a snowy trail, we arrived at the base of a virtual *skyscraper* of ice. What in summer was a 70-foot-high waterfall cascading off a cliff had been caught by winter in stop-motion. It resembled a gentle staircase like a sidewalk resembles a wall. I could feel my heart pounding

madly as we gazed up at it. But then the ice tools came out, and, with Jon leading, we began to inch our way up with much grunting and panting and thunking of ice axes.

As recently as 40 years ago, this pitch would probably have lain beyond the technical ability of the most expert mountaineer. Since the late 1960s, however, ice climbing has undergone advances in equipment that allow the climber to scale sheer walls of ice like Spiderman. You carry a short, sharp axe in each hand that you swing into the frozen surface for handholds, and your boot toes are mounted with a set of sharp metal points to kick into the ice for toe-

Securely roped in, an ice climber leads an ascent of Habegger Falls, Bishop Creek Canyon, in California's Sierra Nevada Mountains.

hugging the surface of a towering frozen face does not appeal to everyone, and it can intimidate even the most enthusiastic beginner with its bewildering array of safety equipment — ropes, harnesses, ice screws — and techniques. And it can take a lot of dedication simply to get to the places where you can climb ice. Much ice climbing requires a hike into the mountains in winter, although if you are lucky enough to reside in the right place, you can spot some frozen waterfalls from major highways and walk to them easily.

Mountaineers climb ice walls by necessity if the ice stands between them and the peak of a mountain they're bound to ascend. But another school seeks out steep ice for the sheer pleasure of it. You perform a kind of dance that you choreograph yourself and, as you climb a pillar of ice, you embrace winter more intimately than at

holds. Together, they allow you to cling to the vertical surface.

Though the sport has boomed in the last 30 years, it still counts only a small band of devotees. The thought of

Rugged, insulated boots keep feet warm, stand up to the rigors of climbing, and accept crampons, the sharp steel spikes that allow you to scale walls of ice. The toothed, drop-forged front points of the crampons on the left boot are designed to excel on especially steep, hard ice.

any other time.

Note that this chapter cannot possibly replace a competent and experienced ice-climbing instructor. No beginner should attempt to climb on ice without expert tutelage in fundamental rock climbing technique, including belays and safety techniques. The ice climber should also be familiar with avalanche precaution, evaluation of ice conditions, and general mountain safety. For more detail, consult *Ice World* by Jeff Lowe or *Modern Rope Techniques in Mountaineering* by Bill March. See Sources & Resources, where you'll also find information on contacting ice-climbing or mountaineering clubs.

Having driven the front-points of his crampons into the ice, a climber swings his ice axe to make his way up a particularly steep pitch.

ICE-CLIMBING HISTORY

True mountaineering — climbing mountains for sport — started in the late 1700s in the French and Swiss Alps. From the beginning, mountaineers had to find ways to conquer steep ice and snow without slipping. The earliest tools for these activities

On walls like this, always three points (two feet and a hand, or vice versa) imbedded in the ice.

consisted of a long staff equipped with a spike on one end and a pike-like head on the other (the ice axe) and a set of metal points called crampons that climbers lashed to their heavy leather boots to give them purchase on the slippery slopes.

For more than a century, mountaineers ascended steep, icy slopes by chopping steps with their big ice axes to create an impromptu staircase. This required a tremendous amount of labor, not to mention arm strength, and progress was slow. Chopping steps on extremely steep ice required inhuman energy, and much of this sort of climbing was perforce done on the fairly gentle surfaces of glaciers.

BECOMING SCHOOLED ON ICE

Once again, we emphasize that ice climbing is not a sport that you should simply go out and try on your own. One way to learn is to find someone who is an experienced ice climber and ask for a lesson. Ice climbers often are eager to introduce neophytes to their sport. Outing clubs and university outdoor programs are other places to look for ice-climbing instruction, which is often offered at only a nominal charge.

Intensive instruction for both beginning and advanced ice climbers is offered by formal mountaineering and ice-climbing schools in the more mountainous regions of the United States. These range from a 1- or 2-day introductory program to extensive courses lasting a week or more that include significant ascents of peaks like Mount Rainier and the Grand Teton, at prices from about $185 to $1,000. Depending on the nearby mountain ranges and the weather, they are offered in both winter and summer. See Sources & Resources for a listing of some of the ice-climbing schools in the United States.

This changed in the
1960s when mountaineers
developed tools that
allowed them to cling to
a vertical face. Crampons
already existed that featured
steel teeth projecting straight
out from the toe to allow the
climber to kick directly into an
ice face. The breakthrough that
opened up the world of ice
climbing was the development by
Yvon Chouinard of a short ice axe
with a "drooped" pick that stuck
easily when hammered into the
ice, enabling the climber essentially to hang from the ice face
with one in either hand.

"With one of these modified
tools in each hand," writes Jeff Lowe,
"normally angled ice slopes suddenly
became much less difficult....the way
was now open for extended climbs on
extremely steep [or even] vertical ice."

SAFETY EQUIPMENT

Besides ice axes and crampons for
the ascent, the ice climber needs a
wide array of safety equipment to
catch her in the event of a fall.
Climbers typically wear a harness
around their waist and
thighs like rock
climbers, to which
they tie a
standard
160-foot
climbing
rope. The lead
climber carries an
assortment of ice
screws (threaded
metal tubes) or
other hardware to
bore into the ice
as anchors for the
rope. As she
ascends, the lead
climber periodi-
cally places one
of the ice screws
in the ice and,
using a metal
loop called a
carabiner,
clips the
rope to
the ice
screw.

The lead
climber then
continues upward, as
the rope runs through
the carabiner. If the lead climber
should lose footing or handholds and
fall, she will plummet past the ice
screw until the rope becomes taut
and catches the fall. Down below, the
far end of the rope is managed by the
second climber who "belays" the
leader by playing out slack as the

leader climbs, and clamps down on the rope with various techniques should the leader fall.

After the leader has reached the top of the pitch, she sets up another belay and manages the rope for the second climber from above. The second climber also removes the ice screws and carabiners on the way.

TECHNIQUE

Ice climbing requires techniques keyed to the varying ice conditions and slopes that you'll find in the mountains. While the sport, in the mind of the American public at least, has become associated with frozen waterfalls or other near-vertical surfaces, much ice climbing takes place on gentler ice slopes and glaciers. The difference between the two resembles the difference between technical rock climbing — working your way straight up a cliff — and mountaineering, when, to get to the top of a mountain, sometimes you're walking across a flat area and sometimes up a gentle slope and at other times you're climbing a cliff.

For gentler slopes, ice climbers use their crampons in what's known as the "French technique." This consists of putting boot soles and crampon points flat on the surface of the ice. Depending on the hardness of the ice, the French technique is effective for angles up to about 45 degrees.

On steeper slopes, climbers use the "German technique," also known as "front-pointing." Here they kick with the two front points of their crampons straight into the ice surface and stand on the crampon as if on a step. A blend of the French and German methods is called the "American technique."

On moderately sloped ice, climbers need only one standard ice axe, but as the angle steepens they'll use two. These are chosen by personal preference from a wide assortment of long- and short-shafted ice axes and "ice hammers." A hammer sports an ice-axe pick on one end of its head and a hammerhead on the other.

On The Ice

Thus equipped, you start climbing. You walk up to the wall of ice and "place" your first ice axe or hammer by choosing a spot above your head but not quite at your arm's full reach. Aim carefully at the spot and place the axe with one blow, if possible. It will resound with a satisfying thunk as it bites into good ice; bad ice sounds hollow. You plant your other axe, then look for a spot — preferably a little knob of ice — on which to place the front points of one set of crampons. As you step your weight onto it, they'll sink into the ice. If you can't find a knob, you have to give a firm but not violent kick to set the points. Too hard of a kick and you'll shatter the ice and lose purchase. Similarly, set the points of the other crampon, move one axe and then the other, and up you go.

As you move, you should always keep three points (two feet and a hand, or vice versa) in contact with the ice. Place only one crampon or one axe at a time.

My experience as a rank beginner was neither this simple nor graceful. Jon climbed easily up the first pitch of about 20 feet and rested on a ledge, belaying me from the top. I walked up to the foot of the ice wall. I was already partway up the side of a canyon; behind me I could hear the rush of the stream far below filling winter's frozen silence. I already felt a long way off the ground.

On steep pitches ice climbers rope up using a system of metal clips, called carabiners (below), that allow ropes to be secured to ice screws, the equivalent of the rock climber's pitons and chalks.

I swung my first axe. The ice shattered into chips and sounded hollow. I bashed around a good bit and shattered a lot of ice before I heard the right sort of thunk. I placed the second one, and then my crampons. I tried to move the first axe. It was stuck in the ice. I pulled and wrenched at it, taking care not to twist the axe and possibly bend or snap the pick, before I finally managed to extract it.

Already, just a few feet off the ground, I had started to pant with the exertion. But the ice seemed secure and I did, in fact, feel like a fly clinging easily to a wall. I was moving in a dimension where I'd never moved before.

By the time I reached the ledge I was eager for the rest. But that first pitch turned out to be a warm-up; the next loomed overhead much higher

Ascending steep ice on Fickle Finger of Fate, Patagonia, Chile. Climbers need not range this far abroad to find challenging ice.

and considerably steeper — close to 80 degrees, just short of vertical. It reminded me of one of the huge columns of the Parthenon. Jon instructed me to keep my heels low as I climbed instead of trying to stand on my tiptoes, so my calves wouldn't tire so easily. Once more, Jon started up, moving quickly, his broad shoulders working hard, as I belayed him from below. He reached a ledge at the top and set up for me.

I started up the second pitch. I bashed with my axes and crabbed with my crampons before I was able to find good purchase on the steeper ice. After 10 feet, I was panting like a sprinter. After 25 feet, my arms were trembling with exertion. I didn't have the strength to keep my axe pick straight as I hammered it into the ice, so it glanced off sideways and split off plates of ice. I heard them tumbling

down the frozen waterfall and shattering on the ground below.

"Do a monkey hang!" Jon shouted down to me.

This is a technique where the climber relaxes his grip on the axe handles and hangs from the attached nylon-web loops, taking some of the weight off his feet. I followed Jon's advice and caught my breath. I didn't dare look down.

"Remember the beer and pretzels back in the car!" he shouted.

That provided the incentive I needed to hack and kick my way to the waterfall's summit. Once there I looked out over the treetops and across the canyon to the snowy peaks above me and down into the fog-shrouded valley far below. I felt on top of the world.

CURLING AND BARREL JUMPING

Here are two ice sports that are more esoteric, but no less fun and challenging for their relative rarity in this country. Besides, the more unusual a sport, the more those who are involved are happy to introduce beginners. Ask around and track them down, and your slate of potential winter activities will be richer.

CURLING

Curling comes to us from those same folks who invented golf, another hit-your-mark game: the Scots. It's easy to picture a group of bored lairds skidding rocks about on a frozen pond, first trying to outmatch one another's accuracy, then devising a way to keep score. Incidentally, the Dutch challenge the Scots' claim and, in support, note that the earliest depiction of curling is a painting by Pieter Brueghel, c. 1550, showing huntsmen looking down upon a frozen lake with skaters in the background and curlers in the foreground.

The non-winter sport to which curling is most akin is bocce. In both, the object is to propel one or more of your playing pieces closest to the target. Again like bocce, only those pieces nearer than any of your opponents' score points. It's a game of strategy in which good players are adept at blocking each other's shots with their own pieces, or knocking the other players' pieces out of scoring position.

In curling, the playing pieces are 16 stones, machined into flattened spheres about 1 foot wide, 4 inches

release, the player uses the handle to spin the stone, either "inside" (counterclockwise) or "outside" (clockwise), causing it to bend, or "curl," in that direction as it travels.

For formal competitions, the "sheet," or playing field, is usually laid on a rink. It's 146 feet long and a bit less than 16 feet wide. At either end are four concentric circles ranging from 1 foot to 12 feet in diameter, which serve as targets and are called "houses."

A curler "delivers" a stone down the ice toward the opposite "house," or target. Her teammate is poised to follow the stone and commence sweeping at the shouted command of the "skip," or captain.

high, and weighing 44 pounds. To the top of each is bolted a grip that looks something like a teakettle handle. On

DID YOU KNOW

While there are about 15,000 curlers in the United States, an estimated 1 million people are active in the sport in Canada. There, televised matches draw ratings comparable to hockey.

The captain, or "skip," of each four-person team determines the order of play, calls for inside or outside spin depending on the placement of the opponents' stones, and, perhaps most important, analyzes the changing condition of the ice. Machine-made rinks are purposely "pebbled" with small bumps to provide the traction a stone needs to curl.

That's where the sweepers come in. As the curler throws his stone, his two teammates race ahead of it with brooms, brushing the ice in its path according to shouted orders of the skip. If the stone is losing

3 4 5 6 7 8 9 10 11 12 13 14 15 16   1 2 3 4 5
3 4 5   7

Curlers throw their stones back and forth from one end of a 146-foot-long rink to the other. When all 16 stones (8 per team) have been thrown in one direction and a score recorded, a new round, or "end," begins and the stones are thrown back in the opposite direction.

velocity and beginning its curl too early, the skip calls for furious sweeping to maintain its pace; conversely, with a stone moving too fast to catch the pebbling, the skip calls the sweepers off.

Homemade Curling

Pared to its essence, curling is just sliding stuff at a target. This is not to suggest it isn't a game of skill — indeed, it has been called "chess on ice" — but to encourage you to use your imagination to create "sandlot" versions on your local pond or recreational rink. This can be as simple as placing a pair of extra gloves at some distance and aiming for them with flat-bottomed rocks of roughly equal size. It's a game that, for obvious reasons, kids love.

More competitive adults might wish more uniformity in their

?

DID YOU KNOW

Curling was a demonstration sport in the Winter Olympics of 1924, 1932, 1988, and 1992. Finally, after knocking on the Olympic door for seven and a half decades, curling officially becomes a medal event in 1998.

The "skip" calls on his teammates to sweep ahead of the stone to help maintain its momentum and keep it from curling off the desired course.

"stones." Fill 1-gallon plastic milk jugs with water and freeze; an advantage is that the handle is already there. If you're ambitious, you can pour ready-mix cement into 2-pound coffee cans and insert a metal L-brace as the cement sets up. For your targets, etch concentric circles in the ice with string and two nails.

Finally, introduce brooms. Outdoor ice, with its natural bumps and occasional snow cover, will quickly reveal to you the advantages of skilled sweeping.

BARREL JUMPING

If you're looking for a winter sport where you can quickly achieve a national ranking, consider barrel jumping. You'll instantly be in the top thirty, since fewer than that number of people in the United States regularly vie in organized contests.

On the other hand, you must be willing to fly a couple dozen feet at about 25 miles per hour and land on ice.

Barrel jumping originated in Holland in the mid-nineteenth century, as informal leaping on skates over natural obstacles such as tree trunks frozen into the surface of Amsterdam's canals. It took a while to reach North America, where the first World Championship was held in 1950 at Grossinger's resort in the Catskill Mountains in upstate New York. Today, it is most popular in Canada, no doubt because ice rinks are more common in our hockey-crazed northern neighbor. Canada is also home to the world's only institute of barrel-jumping higher education, the Speedskating and Barrel Jumping School, run by Gilles Leclerce in St. Bruno, Quebec.

In barrel jumping, fiberboard cylinders 30 inches long and 16 inches in diameter are set side-to-side; if, as is usually the case, the venue is a hockey rink, the row of barrels begins at about the blue line and points toward the opposite corner. Jumpers build up speed by circling the three-quarters of the rink ahead of the barrels; some favor several increasingly large orbits while others prefer one careen about the area. The jumper then makes his approach and leaps. The rules at this point are simple: You're given three tries at each number of barrels; touching one results in no jump; clearing them all is a go.

Perhaps surprising, jumpers who do clear the barrels more often land on their skates, although spills are not uncommon. Injury is uncommon; because most of the jump's momentum is in the forward direction, botched landings almost always result in minimal impact and a long slide, with damage limited to the jumper's dignity.

Don't plan on making the books; the longest jump, 18 barrels, was made by Canadian Yvon Jolin in

DID YOU KNOW

Barrel jumpers wear long-bladed skates similar to those of speed skaters, with the blades offset to the left of the centerline. This helps maintain equilibrium while making the tight turns of the counterclock-wise speed-building run on a hockey rink. The lean through these turns is so extreme that the boots of non-offset skates can touch the ice.

1985, and prior to that the 17-barrel mark had held for two decades. Also, don't plan on cashing in on your fame if you do score big. A few of the dozen or so organized events in the United States and Canada offer prize money, but it tops out at about $1,000. Commercial endorsement opportunities are rare, although Ben Sipes, president of the United States Barrel Jumping Association, told us that he did appear in the early 1980s in a television commercial for Barrelhead, a regional bottler of root beer.

Since we had Ben on the line, we asked him for a few tips before we tried out barrel jumping on our local hockey rink. "Wear a lot of pads," he advised. Ben dons a football girdle for spinal protection, along with cushioning on the knees and elbows, and a helmet, mandatory in competitions.

Good advice, but we were more interested in clearing that elusive 19th barrel. What's the secret? we demanded.

Ben gave it a moment of thought. "Go fast," he said, "and jump high."

WINTER CAMPING

12

A typical response from a neophyte when you suggest they leave their warm living room and go sleep in the snow in the middle of January is a quizzical, you-must-be-joking look. The second response is, "Why on earth would I want to do that?"

There are many reasons, beginning with those shared with camping in the summer: to escape from the confusion and buzz of modern life, to bring yourself more closely in touch with the natural world, to restore a long-lost sense of self-reliance. But the big difference between winter and summer camping is that in winter everything *intensifies* — the pleasures of the outdoors become more

profound, the discomforts more acute.

Even hard-core winter campers draw the line somewhere; one expert winter camper we consulted says he heads for a heated cabin and a mug of hot spiced wine as soon it gets colder than 15 below zero.

The axiomatic rule of all outdoor activities, summer as well as winter, is: You do not have to do this. In our pursuits, we seek fun and recreation, not misery. We've learned to draw the line; in the case of winter camping, we won't hesitate to fold the tent or even postpone the trip if it's too cold.

But you'll be surprised at how comfortable you can be camping in the snow at, say, 20 degrees if properly equipped. Indeed, you may find such a temperature quite felicitous; raise it 10 degrees, and you'll start to sweat. Some enthusiasts with good circulatory systems find winter camping more comfortable than their summer outings, because in summer they sweat while sleeping inside the steamy tent in which they've zipped themselves to escape the bugs. This is another advantage of winter camping: No clouds of mosquitoes or blackflies send you fleeing madly through the woods, slapping at face and legs.

You don't have to slog mile after mile into the forest in order to encounter the solitude of winter. Campsites and trails close to home that seem busy and crowded in the summer will appear remote and deserted in winter.

However far you go, you'll discover that the rewards are profound: total immersion in the glories of winter; the silence and frozen solitude of forest and mountains; the sculptures rendered by nature in snow and ice; a camaraderie that one develops not only with one's companions, but with any other warm-blooded life that remains active in the forest. And you'll discover a peacefulness in winter camping that you'll find at no other time of the year.

■

It's unavoidable: You need a lot of gear to camp in the winter. You must carry your own fire, warmth, and food. On most trips, winter campers tote everything they need in backpacks, but for long trips some choose to drag behind them a small toboggan-like sled called a *pulk*.

LOCOMOTION

Virtually all winter campers travel on skis or snowshoes; walking on booted feet through deep snow carrying a heavy pack is a recipe for exhaustion. Your choice of snowshoes or skis depends on personal preference. You'll also find a wide choice of styles of both skis and snowshoes.

For snowshoe choice, see Chapter 2. Like snowshoes, there is no "right" or "wrong" choice of skis but simply different options for different conditions — and there are accompanying

Snug, four-season tents can stand up to nearly anything, even the intense wind and frigid temperatures at 83 degrees south latitude in Antarctica.

trade-offs. The one recommendation we can make with certainty is to avoid a "track" cross-country ski — the kind used on a prepared course. It is too slender, has too much camber (the amount of "bow" from tip to tail), and is not ruggedly built enough for the rigors of backcountry

ski touring, where at times you're apt to bash your skis over rocks and stumps.

Some backcountry ski campers prefer a purebred Telemark ski so they can freely descend the slopes. Others favor an all-around mountaineering ski. The latter glides more easily when you're walking on the flats, but turns less adeptly on the way downhill.

Another major choice is between a "waxable" and "waxless" ski. A waxable ski has a smooth bottom over which you apply a combination of waxes depending on the snow conditions, to allow your ski to "grip" when you kick back or climb uphill. A waxless ski has a bottom that's etched with a pattern — often "fish-scale" scallops — that grips the snow when the ski slides backward, but is smooth enough to allow the ski to glide forward. Generally a waxable ski performs better, uphill and down, than a waxless ski.

We've always chosen a waxable ski, but admit that at times we've found ourselves plenty frustrated trying to find the right wax combination while a friend on waxless skis motors past us up the slope. In mountainous terrain,

we favor "skins," making the choice of waxable versus waxless less crucial. Skins are strips of a felt-like substance that you apply with an adhesive to your ski bottoms when you wish to climb a steep incline, and remove when you reach the top and are ready to ski down.

The waxable/waxless ski debate becomes more critical in flatter parts of the country where efficiency of glide is a more significant issue.

TENTS

For shelter, choose a tent that withstands wind and is easy to erect. Manufacturers refer to "three-season tents" and "four-season tents," with the latter appropriate for winter use. You can use a three-season tent in

The North Face VE-25, a four-season four-person mountaineering tent designed to withstand anything winter can throw at it.

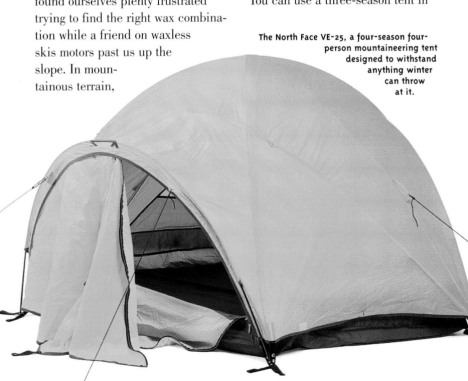

The quinzhee (left) is an easily-constructed Native American shelter made by shoveling snow into a mound, then tunneling in. Snow is a better insulator than nylon, though a quality four-season tent is another option.

the winter, but be aware that, unlike a four-season tent, it's probably not designed for very cold temperatures and heavy gales. The smaller the tent, the warmer you'll be, but you'll sacrifice living space. My four-season tent is a snug little tunnel of cheery yellow fabric in which the body heat of two occupants raises the indoor temperature a good 15-20 degrees. Look for a tent with a vestibule over the door in which you can store your wet gear or, if necessary, cook in inclement weather.

Some veteran winter campers give their tent the "mitten test." It passes if you can erect it without removing your mittens. This is an important consideration if you plan

on camping in frigid temperatures.

SNOW STRUCTURES

We here in the balmier regions of North America think of the igloo as the traditional everyday shelter of the Inuits of the Arctic. In fact, in most of the Arctic the igloo was used only as a temporary or emergency shelter when the Inuit were on a hunting expedition or traveling; otherwise they lived in houses of stone and sod that were bermed into the earth.

Some outdoor writers put forth the igloo as a winter-camping shelter for backcountry travel for we Southerners, too. This is realistic only if you have plenty of patience and practice in building one. Early explorers reported that it took two Eskimo hunters about an hour of hard, skilled labor cutting and fitting the

blocks to build a small snow house.

The Quinzhee

The quinzhee is a lesser-known but

SNOW HOUSE SAFETY

The possibility of the collapse of a competently-built snow shelter is far less than it would intuitively seem. However, the key word is "competent."

Before attempting to build in the backcountry any structure more complex than a tent berm, make one in your backyard. Observe it over several days; when you've succeeded in erecting a quinzhee or snow cave that withstands the elements for that period, you are ready to try it where it counts.

Even so, in the field you should always have your shovel or other digging implement inside and close to hand. This is a precaution not so much against collapse but drifting in. If the elements block your entrance you won't likely be trapped, but it's nice to have a tool to help clear your way out.

Ventilation is mandatory if you use any artificial heat source, even a candle, and recommended in all snow dwellings. Snow in its natural state has some breatha-

bility, but your body warmth alone may cause the interior to melt and freeze, reducing its permeability. Ventilation doesn't measurably affect coziness and is easy to provide. Simply poke a hole in ceiling or wall with a branch, ski pole, or kitchen utensil. A diameter of an inch is sufficient; check occasionally to ascertain it is not blocked by blow-over.

In any structure, avoid sitting or reclining directly on snow. Your body is 67 degrees warmer than a frozen surface, a great enough difference to conduct heat at a surprisingly rapid rate even through clothing. Increase the barrier between body and snow by sitting on a folded blanket, sleeping bag or pad, spare parka, or your pack.

Finally, children should never be allowed to play in or on a snow shelter without a vigilant adult present. If you've erected the structure in your unfenced yard and the neighborhood kids are frequent visitors, post a sign and spread the word among them: You'd be happy to give a free tour to any kid and one of his parents.

more easily constructed snow house that was used by the Native Americans of the North Woods. It can be built with most types of snow, and even works well with powder.

Begin by mounding a pile of snow 6 feet high and 10 feet in diameter. If the snow is soft, you can pack it a bit, but the act of digging and piling breaks down the structure of individual flakes and helps them bond more firmly together. By the next morning, your pile will have consolidated, and the process can take as little as an hour if it's cold enough. Heavier snow will settle and bond even more quickly; about the only variety to avoid is very wet snow, which may freeze solid.

To fashion the quinzhee, dig your way inside the pile, and continue to hollow it out. Pass the dislodged snow out to your companions to be hauled off, and as the interior takes shape, swap your shovel for a hand-held garden spade. The dome is the correct thickness when outside light just begins to turn the ceiling from opaque to translucent.

The igloo, however alluring in our imaginations, requires enough skill and time to build to make it impractical for most winter campers.

Berms

Berms are snow walls which are usually built to serve as windbreaks for overnight camping in tents. A berm need not be elaborate; a pile of snow four feet high and six feet long will offer significant protection to all but the largest tents.

Digging down into the snow of the tent site will effectively increase the berm's height by lowering the tent. Once that's done, pile your berm with a camp shovel. If the snow is powdery, some minor packing may be necessary, but the act of digging into the virgin powder breaks up the individual snow crystals to cause a natural increase in density.

When the berm is complete, set up your tent with its back to the barrier and the entrance facing away, for extra protection against the wind. Note, however, that this is not the desired configuration if you don't choose to build a berm. In that case, the entrance should face perpendic-

The snow cave can provide snug, relatively spacious living quarters when snow conditions are right, and you're planning to stay put for several days.

ular to the prevailing gusts, to avoid snowdrift blockage.

Snow Trenches

Building a snow trench is relatively quick, easy, and foolproof. It can serve instead of a tent for sleeping quarters, if you don't mind walls of snow. Some winter campers prefer them. The simplest trench can be dug out with skis, hands, or a pot lid, and you can also kick snow out with your boots. The deeper you can make it, the more protective the trench will be; a couple of feet is the minimum practical depth. When digging, make one end lower than the other, to act as a catch basin for cold air. For single occupancy, a trench three feet wide by seven or eight feet long is more

than sufficient. Position it so it is perpendicular to the prevailing gale.

To keep drifting snow out and body warmth in, your trench will need a roof. Deadfall pine boughs can be propped in a triangular pattern to form a peaked ceiling, and among this natural material you can also incorporate your skis or snowshoes.

Better yet, if you are carrying a shovel or saw and the snow is firm, you can turn the trench into a poor person's igloo. Cut blocks two feet to a side and six inches thick and prop them in a peaked-roof pattern. Close one end with a snow block and use your pack for a door on the other, for maximum interior warmth. To keep your butt from chilling, sit on a spare article of clothing or your sleeping pad. This type of trench makes an excellent emergency shelter that can be quickly and easily constructed.

Snow Caves

Snow caves require deep, firm snow. For this reason, people build them mainly in the high mountains where the snow has blown into large drifts. You want a depth of at least five feet of dense snow, preferably on the leeward side of a hill or ridge. The slope should be no greater than 25 degrees, however, to avoid the possibility of avalanche.

To construct a snow cave, tunnel in about two feet on a slight rise to allow cold air to flow down and out of your completed cave. Then begin carving upward at a greater angle; your object is to create a dome that's about six feet wide at the base. Plan for a ceiling at least a foot thick, for insulative warmth.

You might want to include in your design a snow bench on which you can sit while dining or reading. Note that a snow cave requires several hours of hard, wet work to construct, and snow conditions must be appropriate. It's best constructed only if you plan to stay in one spot for several days, or in an emergency or very difficult weather conditions.

Snow caves can withstand the most hellacious wind and cold. They are so snug that screaming winds outside can barely be heard, and the body-heat of several occupants is not only enough to heat them to a toler-

able temperature but can actually slightly melt the walls. If you cook in them, you must create an airhole in the roof for ventilation.

STOVES

A reliable stove is a crucial item on a winter-camping trip, not only to heat your food but to melt snow to provide drinking water. You'll find a wide variety, but pay particular attention to weight, ease of operation, and heat output. A weak stove in winter will cause you no end of inconvenience as you wait for what seems like hours for it to melt a pot of snow. For this reason, some winter-camping experts recommend that you steer clear of the type of stove that comes with a pressurized gas cartridge, because in very cold weather, or when the cartridge is low, the heat output lessens. On the other hand, these stoves are convenient, light, and relatively safe, since you don't have to fill them with fuel yourself. They are most suitable for short trips, or as an emergency stove that takes up little pack room during day trips.

European winter campers favor alcohol-fueled stoves. These are safe and reliable, though alcohol is bulky compared to other fuels. In this country, most winter campers prefer white-gas or kerosene models. Both have a high heat output but tend to be trickier to use and are potentially dangerous, especially the white-gas models, due to the volatility of the

taken to provide adequate ventilation against invisible and odorless carbon monoxide fumes. A stove should never be lit inside a tent .

Each trip and party will vary, but, when melting snow and cooking on a winter-camping expedition, experts figure on using a little more than a quarter of a pint of white gas or kerosene per person per day.

As a precautionary note, consider the time our white-gas stove exploded in a fireball on a remote beach in northern

A reliable, powerful stove like this Swiss-made Sigg Fire Jet is as important for melting snow for drinking water as it is for cooking.

fuel and the possibility of spills.

No stove, and especially a white-gas model, should be used inside a tent unless there is absolutely no other choice. All care should be

Greenland one sunny July morning at 4 a.m. We somersaulted backward in surprise, lucky not to have been injured in so remote a place. It was our own fault; we hadn't properly maintained a gasket that began to leak, and then we over-pressurized the stove because we were in a hurry to chow down before we began a long hike down the beach back to an Inuit village. We liked the stove despite that eyebrow-singeing explosion and bought the same model again, but we now keep a closer eye on that gasket and hold the pressure down.

The Kelty Polaris is a four-season sleeping bag filled with Polar Guard synthetic insulation and rated effective to minus 15 degrees F.

SLEEPING BAGS

We still don't know of any perfect choice for a sleeping bag for winter camping. Here you confront the same dilemma — down versus artificial fill — as with outdoor clothing (see Chapter 14): A down bag is light and warm but becomes almost useless when wet because the down collapses. An artificial-fill bag retains its loft when wet but is bulky and heavy. Some down bags now come with a waterproof but breathable covering, but we've seen mixed reviews on

---

TECHNIQUE TIP

GEARING DOWN

If you are picnicking with kids (or with fumble-fingered adults like us, for that matter), tie or tape 18-inch lengths of red ribbon to small items such as compass, Swiss Army knife, and sunglasses. When a tot drops her Sierra cup in deep powder, you'll recover it instantly, instead of burrowing about while muttering Anglo-Saxonisms.

how effectively these bags keep dry on extended or particularly soggy trips. Other winter campers swear that with a little care and caution, you can keep a down bag dry under almost any circumstances.

Your choice also depends on the climate in which you'll camp — whether you'll likely encounter wet and mild winter weather or cold and dry. Whichever your choice, don't stint on warmth. Manufacturers give ratings to their sleeping bags according to the minimum temperature at which it will still provide comfort, but these are general guidelines and some people sleep "warm" and some "cold." As a rule of thumb,

---

GEAR TALK

LUGGAGE CRAFT

Backpack considerations differ in winter. If you are skiing, leave the external-frame pack at home; most are too wide to avoid banging your elbows while you pole. An internal-frame pack also hugs your body more closely and won't swing about in an unwieldy fashion and knock you off balance as you turn on skis.

While it's a good practice to stow the heavy gear toward the top of an external-frame pack, it's best to stash the hardware first (the tent, not the sleeping bag, goes in the bottom in an internal-frame pack). This lowers your center of gravity, a distinct advantage when skiing. An added advantage is easier access to the clothing on top; on a typical day, changes in the weather and the exertion of the trek mean more frequent doffing and donning of duds.

Internal-Frame Pack

Upper Straps: raise or lower pack on your back

Padded Shoulder Straps: adjust for comfort

Sternum Strap: relieves pressure on shoulders

Compression Straps: cinch bulk of load close to body

Posture Pad: adjust up or down to fit your back

Lumbar Pad

Padded Hip Belt: with stabilizer straps

figure that about 6 inches of loft ("loft" refers to the thickness of a sleeping bag when it lies on the ground) will keep you warm to about 20 degrees, while 8 inches of loft is comfy down to about zero.

We recommend a "mummy bag" rather than the old rectangular bags that were popular years ago. A mummy bag hugs your body so that you don't have to warm up a lot of empty air space. You should nevertheless buy a mummy bag with enough roominess to wear heavy clothing inside it if necessary. Some people like a longer bag so they can store their boots at the bottom to avoid placing their feet in frozen leather in the morning. Also, a hood on your bag is a must for winter camping. For particularly cold conditions, some winter campers carry two lighter bags and stuff one inside the other to make a double bag.

Don't even think about camping in the snow without an insulated sleeping pad, preferably a full-length one. I tried it once years ago in the White Mountains of New Hampshire out of sheer ignorance and even inside the tent I felt like a sidewalk-market fish on a bed of shaved ice. I finally dragged my rigid-framed pack into the tent and slept on top of it. It was like lying on the rungs of a ladder, but at least I was warmer

Other gear that you'll want, besides the standard clothing items in Chapter 14, includes a pair of down booties or overboots to wear

A hut at Willamette Pass, Willamette National Forest, in Oregon's Cascade Region. For many, the sensible alternative to hard-core winter camping is hut-to-hut skiing.

around camp. You'll find it an indescribable luxury at the end of the day to unfetter your feet from your cold, hard, wet ski boots and slip them into a pair of soft, warm booties.

WHERE AND WHEN TO GO

A positive, if paradoxical, approach for the beginning winter camper is to schedule your first trip for spring, when the days are warmer and longer. With this experience under your belt, you'll be more predisposed to try camping in the dead of winter, where you may encounter truly frigid temperatures and must retire to your sleeping bag as darkness falls early.

terrain, consult the local Forest Service or other agencies who provide avalanche forecasts (see page 207).

Getting There

Traveling on skis with a heavy pack, you can figure to make

A well-chosen winter campsite. High in the stormy Patagonia Range a snow drift has been employed as both a windbreak for a tent and the site for a snow cave.

An introductory alternative is to begin with a trip to a hut or cabin, and advance to a tent on your next outing, which is bound to be more challenging. You might even spend a January night with your tent pitched in your own backyard; however, you'll miss out on the serene glories of the wilderness in winter (the payoff), but you'll get a feel for the difficulties imposed by the cold.

The same approach applies to routes and destinations: Start small, and work your way up, doubly so if you are bringing kids. A 2-mile ski to a lakeshore, frozen waterfall, or serene forest glen might make for a good first trip. Such a "shakedown cruise" helps you figure out how to do it, what equipment you need, and what techniques work best for you.

Be sure to carefully check the weather forecasts before you go and, if you expect to travel in mountain

between 5 and 12 miles per day, depending on the terrain and your fitness. In steep country covered with deep snow, you might make fewer miles, while on a packed trail on the flats you'll traverse considerably more.

Time of day will also affect your pace, especially in spring, when the early-morning snow is firm and fast underfoot and the snow late in the day slushy and slow. In mid-winter, on the other hand, you might want to travel later in the day when the sun is higher and warmer.

Remember that it helps to keep a steady pace, take turns breaking trail, and pay attention to where you are. Even in cold temperatures you'll quickly work up a sweat under a heavy pack, making it important to shed extra layers of clothing before you become drenched, because the perspiration will chill you when you stop. You'll also lose a remarkably large quantity of water through sweat and breathing when working hard in the winter; you must drink often and copiously to take on the gallon of fluid per day your body requires. Monitor the color of your urine: If it is dark, you are not sufficiently hydrated.

Plan for plenty of time to set up camp at the end of the day; chores take longer in winter camping, and darkness falls early and swiftly. Stop well before the sun drops; the instant it does, the temperature will plummet, and by this point you'll want to be warm and set up for the night.

Selecting a Campsite and Making Camp

Some winter campers prefer to camp on snow, some on dry ground if they can find it. Snow offers a nice soft surface on which to sleep, and an easy medium in which to drive your tent stakes, but it also chills the floor of your tent more than dry, grassy ground and you constantly track snow into the tent.

Look for a patch of dry ground on a south slope, in the shelter of conifer trees, or where the wind has scoured away the snow (this latter site is bound to be gusty, however). Some campers shovel down to dry ground if the snow cover is thin.

If you pitch a camp where the snow is soft and fluffy, pack it down with skis or tramp it with your boots.

Avoid situating your tent beneath the boughs of a snow-laden tree that might slough its load on you in the middle of the night or, if you're in the mountains, at the base of an obvious avalanche path.

Pitch your tent as you would in summer, but unless the snow is firm, you'll need wider stakes than you would use in earth. Some winter campers jam their skis and poles into the snow for stakes, others carry "snow stakes" with a somewhat wider blade, available at mountain shops and some camping stores. If you anticipate windy conditions, you can build a windbreak of snow around your tent or dig it down into the snow. Some experts suggest placing the windbreak at the same distance from the tent as the windbreak is high; this spacing will capture the blowing snow before it piles on your tent.

You may also dig a "kitchen pit," an excavation away from the wind and equipped with little niches and shelves on which to place your stove and food, as well as benches. It's easy enough to build a fire on a stamped-out spot (it will sink down into a pit as it burns). A fire adds cheer and warmth to a campsite, but in these days of low-impact camping it's best to avoid one in environmentally sensitive areas. Always use deadfall rather than cutting snags or breaking branches off standing trees, and scatter ashes and half-burned sticks before you leave.

When setting up your camp, scan the area for a spot to use as a latrine. It should be at least 100 yards away from a stream or lake, and well away from any obvious trails or campsites that hikers might use the next summer. If the snowpack is shallow and the ground unfrozen, you can dig a "cat-hole." Otherwise, bury feces in the snow, choosing the spot with the awareness that they'll melt out in spring and eventually deteriorate.

Toilet paper left on or in the snow will remain at least through the next several summers before it decomposes. Bury, burn, or pack it out in a plastic bag. Some purists use snow instead of toilet paper.

?

DID YOU KNOW

At the moment we're back at the ranch drinking hot toddies, thank you very much, but imagine you are in the field in 50-below weather and seeking amusement. To check the temperature's effect on your hand-eye coordination, practice your curveball against a tree, using an egg. By a marvelous coincidence of nature, the expansion factor of the frozen ovum equals the shell volume. The tree may topple, but the egg won't crack.

Whatever the method, winter campers should be sure to wash their hands with biodegradable soap and water, or antiseptic cleaning pads, after using the latrine.

After You've Made Camp

Immediately after making camp you should change from the wet, cold clothes you used on the trail to layers that are dry and warm. Ignore this advice and you'll be shivering within minutes; mind it and that fresh set of long johns, undershirt, socks, and down booties will make you feel that you've donned regal robes. Add a hot drink prepared on your camp stove, and you're in the lap of luxury. Winter camping will make you appreciate more deeply than ever before the profound pleasure of the simplest creature comfort.

Once you've pitched camp and changed clothes, it's time to think about fixing dinner and replenishing your water supply.

Water

You will have saved yourself a lot of work if you have a source of open water nearby. Often, you can use a ski pole or other instrument to break through the ice on a frozen stream or at the edge of a lake to find fresh-water. (This should be done with the utmost caution, because help is a long way away; see page 170 on ice safety.) Otherwise you'll have to melt snow to make water, a task that occupies a lot of time in a winter camp.

Given that fluffy new snow is up to 98 percent air, you'll need to melt many potfuls to get a single pot of water. To quicken the process, begin by pouring some water from your canteen into the pot and then add snow. The older, denser, and "icier" the snow, the more water it contains and the less you'll need.

It's generally wise to let the water boil for at least five minutes to kill any harmful bacteria, regardless of how pure the snow appears. You can also use water-purification tablets, available at camping stores. Snow melted in a pot produces water with a distinctive flat taste. Our friend Mike Sherwood, a veteran winter camper, suggests pouring the meltwater from bottle to

A kitchen counter carved from snow. You can expect to burn twice as many calories traveling and camping in winter as in your day-to-day life.

bottle to reaerate it and improve the flavor or, better, using it to make hot drinks like cocoa.

Once you've provided yourself with a water supply, you must protect the bottles from freezing. When traveling in frigid temperatures, keep a water bottle under your clothing or insulate it well and stow it in your pack. In camp, share your sleeping bag with your canteen. To keep your spare bottles from freezing overnight, Mike suggests wrapping them in Ensolite or other insulating material and burying them upside down in a foot of snow. The snow provides further insulation, and the inverted position prevents the opening from freezing shut.

Cooking

After my first deep-winter camping experience — a week on skis in the Northern Rockies at temperatures from 20 below to 20 above — I returned home and, about to take my first bath in a week, looked in the mirror. While the beard added some new bulk to my face, it appeared that my torso had measurably shrunk. Ever since, I've told people who talk about going on a diet that the fastest way to lose weight is to go winter camping.

You'll burn about twice as many calories traveling and camping in the winter as in your more sedentary day-to-day life.

Figure you'll need at least 4,000 calories per day. The paradox is to stuff enough calories down your gullet while minimizing the expenditure of those calories through the effort of carrying their weight. We know winter campers in the frigid forests of Minnesota and Michigan who solve the problem by toting along several pounds of butter and chopping off great gobs of it into their soup, tea, oatmeal, and pasta, to fuel their internal furnaces. While winter camping, you'll come to understand why Eskimos crave blubber.

The standard dinner for winter campers is either freeze-dried and supplemented by snacks or a one-pot meal of macaroni, rice, or instant potatoes to which you add dried vegetables, dried or canned meats, soup bases, and the like. The advantage of the one-pot approach is that it's fast, simple, and you can easily vary the ingredients to create new combinations. In addition, one-pot meals reduce preparation and cleanup hassle.

The breakfast of choice among winter campers is oatmeal, granola, or (our personal favorite) instant noodles, which we doctor up with butter or cheese. Add to the menu lots of hot drinks such as tea, cocoa, or instant fruit juices, to pre-hydrate you for the day.

Lunch, often eaten on the fly, consists of cheese, bread, crackers, peanut butter, salami, candy bars, granola bars, fruit, and nuts. Some winter campers stop and pull out a stove to brew up hot soup or tea. This makes a welcome and warming break if you don't mind the time and trouble; you can also carry an insulated vacuum bottle of soup or a hot drink prepared in the morning. (If you do, keep in mind that a steel bottle won't break as easily as the plastic-and-glass variety.) Generally,

Skiers on a backcountry tour in the Selkirks, British Columbia, Canada. The warmth of a campfire is especially welcome at 10 below.

figure on a little more than 2 pounds of dry food per person per day, although you should always take extra as emergency rations.

Our friend Dan Mazur, who's climbed both Mount Everest and K2, once showed up for a day of hard climbing on Telemark skis in the Bitterroot Mountains with nothing to eat except two dozen giant garlic breadsticks, poking from his pack like a bundle of firewood. While Dan's simple-but-plenty dining philosophy no doubt helped fuel him to the summits of the world's highest peaks, and we have to admit the breadsticks were tasty, it's our philosophy on winter camping trips to indulge ourselves. Use your imagination to

create new and tasty dishes, because when you're out in the frozen woods or mountains, dinner and breakfast are going to be the much-anticipated anchors of your day.

Sleeping

You'll arrive at the perfect sleeping arrangement for winter camping only after plenty of trial and error, and probably a few chilly nights. Here are a few tricks to even out the learning curve:

● Wear only dry clothes to bed, or your sleeping bag will become progressively soggier. If you're cold, don't hesitate to add socks, sweater or pile jacket, and especially a hat. Draw the hood of the sleeping bag

warm bag and try to ignore the need — by having at your side what winter campers call a "pee bottle." This is a widemouthed (and well-marked) bottle used for just that, and emptied in the morning. Devices specially designed for women are available from local outfitters. The Freshette brand device is available from International Sani-Fem Company, Downey, California 90241; 310-928-3435.

A hot drink can be the perfect way to start the day, particularly from the comfort of your sleeping bag.

tightly around your face. In particularly frigid conditions, I drape my parka over the top of the bag for an extra layer.

● Consider eating a snack before bedtime. The digestion process speeds metabolism and keeps you warmer as you sleep.

● Sleep close to the person in the bag beside you and share the warmth. Zip-together bags have advantages when the temperature is moderate, but you can't seal the hood. In extreme frigidity, limit snuggling to the bag-to-bag mode.

● Solve that inevitable middle-of-the-night dilemma — whether to climb out into the freezing air to relieve yourself, or double over in the

WALKING ON
SNOW AND ICE

I t only takes a few steps in really deep, soft snow to understand why snowshoes and skis were invented to help keep you on top. It's an experience more akin to swimming through molasses than to walking. Watch the way dogs and children charge eagerly out into fresh deep snow and instantly bog to a flailing, foot-plunging crawl. After only a few yards, even they are panting heavily.

Skis and snowshoes are the way to travel over soft snow, and skates or crampons are the footgear for flat or sloping ice. Still, there are times when you'll find yourself on booted feet in snow or on ice. Here are a few tricks to help you along.

WALKING IN AND ON SNOW

The most effective technique for walking in snow really hasn't to do with the act of locomotion but with finding the easiest route. Snow conditions vary considerably from place to place and time to time — even within a few yards, or a few minutes. One advantage is to find those places and times that offer the most easily traversed snow.

For example, the snow might lie deep and soft on a cold, shady, north-facing hillside, but on the warmer, sunnier, south-facing slope just over the hill it has either melted away almost entirely or, if it's early morning,

When walking in deep snow that will not support you, use teamwork by moving in single file, with the leader breaking trail and the others following in the increasingly well-packed footsteps.

lingering crust that you can stroll over as if it were a sidewalk.

A few other tricks about route:

● Look for exposed ridgetops where the wind has swept away the snow and left bare ground or only a thin cover of snow. (Beware of overhanging cornices, however, which could break underfoot, dumping you downslope.)

● Large game animals follow trails in the snow, some packed hard enough to form the winter equivalent of a superhighway. If you can find one of these leading in your general direction of travel, take it.

● Avoid the combination of deep snow and heavy brush or tall grass. Not only is it difficult to wend through the brush, but the underlying vegetation forms air pockets under the snow

crusted up under the rays of yesterday's sun and refrozen to provide a firm base for walking. Later on a sunny spring day, you might find that the snow in the middle of a pasture has softened to the point where you wetly sink up to your knees, but in the shady forest the night's cold has left a cover, so that when you break through your foot plunges deeper than if you were walking in a brushless area.

Walking in Snow that Will Not Support Your Weight

The technique for snow that you cannot walk atop depends on its type, as roughly defined by three categories:

In *dry powder* less than a few inches deep you'll usually be able to move at a normal gait, but as little as a half foot can be a wearying impediment.

Nasqually Glacier, Mount Rainier, Washington. Where windswept snow becomes hard-packed, walking can be superior to skiing or snowshoeing. But where crevasses are a possibility, you should be roped up to your partners.

You can shuffle-step or you can high-step to compress the snow. Try both methods and choose the one that works best. For example, if there is an icy base beneath the powder, high-stepping will provide more traction.

In *heavy wet snow* of any appreciable depth, stomping down with each step is the only way to proceed without tiring yourself in short order. This type of snow does have the advantage of providing firm footholds when you are climbing or descending slopes.

Crusted snow with a top layer too weak to support you can be extremely

frustrating. As you lean onto your forward foot it breaks through at the same time that you are working to extract your rear foot. About the only way to ease this tribulation is to take your time and keep from tiring yourself unnecessarily. If the crust is almost strong enough to hold you up, you can try to find a thicker area, then ease yourself up as gently as possible. Proceed with a shuffle step, keeping your weight shifts to a minimum.

TEAMWORK. In any type of snow that will not support you, your party should move in single file, with the leader breaking trail and the others following in the increasingly well-packed footsteps. Take turns on lead, and when the leader's turn is over, send her to the rear, where the trail is most compacted and she can catch her breath. A turn as leader, incidentally, is over when the leader feels tired and asks to be relieved.

your party suc-
cumb to
fatigue a half
mile from your
goal.

Deep snow
on steep open
slopes should
be avoided
altogether (see
pages 204-210
on avalanche
safety). Find
your way
around or, if
conditions war-
rant, turn back.
This is a team
decision, and
the opinions of
more knowl-
edgeable team
members
should carry
the most
weight.

John Viehman climbing on Mount Rainier's hardpack snow, roped up, with
ice axe at the ready for support or self arrest.

Some party members will perforce
be stronger than others, and it is up
to the individual to assess her capa-
bilities.

Move at a pace that is appropriate to the slowest party member,
especially if kids are present. You
will conserve energy and effective-
ness if your moves are steady and
deliberate. Proceeding at a slower
pace and arriving a little later is
superior to hurrying as the day
latens, only to have a member of

Walking on Hardpack Snow

Two snow types provide conditions
on which walking can actually be
superior to both skiing and snowshoeing. After unseasonably warm
temperatures are followed by a cold
front, the resulting crust may be
strong enough to hold up an average
adult (generally, it must be 2 or
more inches thick). And during
spring in high-mountain country,
snow settles and becomes dense
throughout its depth.

Under either of these conditions, skis and snowshoes generally slip and slide, but boots sink in just enough to provide traction. The principal trap on hard-surfaced snow is the annoyance of "post-holing." It

John Viehman using diagonal uphill technique — along with crampons and ice axe — to ascend a steep, icy slope. Resist the urge to lean into the slope: this will only encourage your feet to slide out from under you.

occurs when you least expect it: You are strolling along, take a step, and your leading leg plunges through the surface and buries itself to the groin.

To avoid post-holing on crusted powder, observe the lay of the land and its features. Consider the compass points: When you crest the south face of a ridge, expect thinner crust on the other side, which is subject to less melt-and-freeze.

On dense spring snow, beware of the area immediately around trees. Boughs, especially those of conifers, will have siphoned off some of the snowfall and also shaded the snowpack from the sun's contribution to compacting, rendering it softer and more conducive to post-holing.

Likewise, the sun's warmth against a big rock or a stump will weaken the snow around it and you'll plunge through if you step near. I can't count the times I've floundered with my booted foot jammed down near the base of a stump, my other foot up on the surface of the snow, and a heavy pack on my back pinning me there like a beetle stuck to a corkboard by an entomologist's thumbtack.

Consider using ski poles even if you are not skiing. They'll help you extract yourself from these predicaments, and when you walk, planting them opposite the leading foot with each step, as you do when cross-country skiing, helps you maintain balance, pace, and the rhythm of your winter hike.

WALKING ON HILLS. Dense slippery snow demands healthy respect when you are on a slope. One misstep and you may find yourself skittering down the mountainside toward trees, rocks, or a cliff.

John Viehman and RMI guide demonstrate self-arrest on Mount Rainier. Once mastered, this three-point method of checking an unplanned fall down a snow field is bombproof. It can save your life.

climbers make the kick-step technique more "bombproof." First, let gravity be your assistant by keeping your body parallel to its pull. This can be counterintuitive in that there is a natural tendency to lean forward when ascending and backward on the way down. But if you do, you increase the chance of your feet skidding out from under you.

Second, wear stiff-soled boots. Soft soles curl when toes are kicked in and then bend when you put your weight on them, making it easier for the boot to slip out of the stairstep. (For more on boots, see page 177.)

The kick-step technique will serve well on slopes of moderate declivity, but if your route includes steeper terrain, especially if dotted with rocks or trees, you should possess at least rudimentary moun-

To negotiate a hillside covered with firm snow, build a "staircase" with kick steps. Ascending, cock your foot so the toe is slightly lower than the heel and drive it forward into the surface. On the way down, the move is reversed: With the toe turned slightly upward, ram your heel into the hillside.

Two tips borrowed from mountain

taineering skills. Begin with a text such as *Mountaineering: The Freedom of the Hills* (see Sources & Resources) and supplement with a few lessons from a friend with climbing experience.

Like all safety techniques, self-arrest should be practiced under controlled conditions before you ever have to use it in a fall. To do so, find a steep slope with hardpack snow and wear an outer layer of nylon-based clothing.

Begin without an ice axe. Fall deliberately, roll, and use hands and feet to arrest. It is essential that you are comfortable with your ability before you take up the axe. If not used with care, this sharp implement can be more dangerous than the fall itself.

Start low on the hill and work your way up. At first your moves will be deliberately thought out; work on them until they become instinctual and repeatedly and quickly bring you to a stop in conditions as difficult as you expect to encounter in the field.

Glissading

The word *glissade* means "slide" in

SELF-ARREST

On Memorial Day weekend a few years ago, I set out for western Montana's Wisherd Ridge for what was to be a casual sledding and Telemark skiing expedition. While "plunge-stepping" down the face of a steep, snow-covered ridge on the way to my destination, I missed a step.

Instantly I was on my back and shooting down the slope. The shiny skin of my garments rocketed me toward looming tree trunks at a speed that dictated serious injury if I collided. As I cascaded downslope, my response was to call on my sledding experience. I used my outstretched gloved hands to steer, aimed just to the left of a Douglas fir, cocked my knees, and plummeted into the tree well at the fir's base. I slammed into the well's downhill wall and came to an abrupt stop, shaken but unharmed.

Reflecting on the incident, I note I made three errors. First, I hadn't considered the possibility of a fall, and thus was mentally unprepared when it did occur. Second, it was avoidable; I should have taken more care in assuring that my heel kicks were vigorous, and my feet cocked so the "stairsteps" were tilted slightly upward. Third, I failed to follow effective self-arrest procedures. The key to self-arrest when sliding down a slope is immediate action; in my case, by the time I gathered

continued on next page

my wits, I was descending so rapidly that self-arrest would have made little difference

If you find yourself in a fall of this sort, flip *without hesitation* onto your stomach. This goes against instinct if there are obstacles downslope that you'd prefer to be able to see, but if you follow through, you'll stop before you reach them. Crab your gloved or mittened fingers and dig them into the snow, while doing a push-up to increase the weight on your hands. At the same time, splay your feet and dig their sides in as well; using your toes instead is an invitation to ankle injury.

When you know in advance that your route includes slopes where a fall is a possibility, consider carrying an ice axe. This climber's implement, shaped roughly like a **T**, is three tools in one: a shaft with an awl at its bottom; a curved, scythe-like blade; and opposite it, a broader blade shaped like a hoe.

As you descend, hold the axe across your body with one hand near the base and the other hand over the bar of the **T**, with the scythe blade up. In a fall, throw both hands to your non-dominant side (the left, if you are a righty), roll onto your stomach, and dig in. This is only one of several ways to employ an ice axe for self-arrest; the mountaineering manuals listed in Sources & Resources describe others.

The ice axe, one of the mountaineer's most versatile tools. The head (above) made up of the pick (left) and the adze (right) and, at the bottom of the shaft, the spike.

French and the way those syllables glide off your tongue is an apt description of how the activity feels on snow.

Technically, "glissade" is a climbing term that refers to descending a snowy mountain slope by sliding on your feet or rear end while braking and steering with an ice axe. In practice, we know people who glissade using a wide variety of simple methods — on bootsoles, snowshoes, and even garbage bags — and choose gentle, safe slopes where an ice axe isn't a necessity. This non-technical glissading is one of those winter activities that can deliver a maximum thrill with a minimum of equipment.

The best season for glissading in the mountains where we live is not winter at all but spring and early summer when the snow has firmed up. Spring's corn snow works perfectly (see Chapter 6). A nice sunny day and a picnic lunch add immeasurably to the experience. Often we combine glissading with an early-summer hike to study the wildflowers that are emerging in the high-mountain meadows.

We picnic in a grassy meadow and study the surrounding terrain where the snow lingers. We choose a snowy slope of moderate pitch that is free of obstacles and drops to a wide, gentle runout that is certain to stop you before you hit anything solid. This runout is your safety, so choose it well. We first climb the lower portion of the slope for a test run to ensure we won't be flying along faster than we'd like and then gradually work our way higher up the slope. This way, everybody in the party seeks their own level of thrill.

The technique couldn't be simpler — you stand on your bootsoles and slide down much like a skier on very short skis. A few secrets you'll eventually discover by trial and error:

● Place one foot in front of the other for stability; you'll prevent yourself from tripping forward when you hit patches of softer snow or flipping backward on slicker snow.

● Spread your feet farther apart and dig in your heels to slow down. Bring your feet closer together and thrust your weight forward for speed.

● You can turn — more or less — by rolling your knees to one side and setting the soles of your boots up on edge, like a skier.

If this *standing glissade* feels too precarious, try the *crouching glissade* by squatting down and dragging a ski pole or even a stick for balance and a brake. Hold it under one arm and rudder as you would with a canoe paddle. A *sitting glissade* is just as it sounds, although the non-technical term known to generations of children is "sliding on your rear." Stretch your legs out in front of you for speed; draw up your knees and place your feet flat on the snow to slow down.

Be especially certain there are no rocks or stumps protruding from the slope. If you run over an obstacle during a fast sitting glissade, you'll gain a new understanding of the phrase "kicked full in the ass."

You can perform a glissade on powdery snow if you're wearing snowshoes (see Chapter 2). The technique is the same as a standing glissade but you must take care that the tips of the shoes don't submarine under the surface and launch you headlong.

Mountaineers can perform glissades on somewhat steeper slopes and firmer snow using an ice axe to check their speed. For more instruction on this technique see *Mountaineering: The Freedom of the Hills* (listed in Sources & Resources).

in the high mountains when I launched into a carefree glissade on a warm summer day off a 13,000-foot peak. I hadn't bothered to check what was below. Suddenly I was flipping onto my belly and wildly clawing with naked fingers in the snow to stop my progress before I careened over a headwall that lay just downslope and had the added attraction of a huge rock pile at its foot. I managed to stop before the

Approaching Fickle Finger of Fate, Patagonia, Chile. The combination of ski poles and crampons makes slick ice like this navigable, even when wearing a heavy pack.

One final note of caution: Glissading is such fun on a warm spring day in snow country, and so easy, that it's also easy to lose your caution in your enthusiasm and suddenly find yourself in deep trouble in the form of an uncontrollable plunge toward a place you don't want to be.

I remember one of my first hikes headwall, but just barely.

This gives a certain resonance to the words of Canadian mountaineering teacher David Begg, who cautions his students with this thumbnail sketch about the perils of glissading: "The fellow's last words were 'Yaba Daba Doo!' right before he slid over the cliff."

WALKING ON ICE

One of my clever boyhood discoveries — at least I thought it clever — was that I could ride a bicycle across the impossibly slick ice of the frozen lake in front of the house in which I grew up. The trick was to start pedaling very slowly so the rear tire wouldn't spin, avoid braking once I did build up a head of steam, and under no circumstances attempt to turn, at pain of having the front wheel skid out to send me sprawling in a clatter of bike and bone to the hard surface.

We bring this up because these same basic principles apply to walking on ice. Ice is quite easy to traverse if it's flat and you avoid sudden moves. You can't push off jauntily to lend a spring to your initial step, as you might on skates; rather, you begin walking at a slow shuffle and build up momentum. You anticipate the need to turn or to stop well in advance, because you must do both gradually. Dogs never do learn the technique; they know how to run at high speed across ice, but watch the wild flailing and skidding when they try to turn or stop to catch a hockey puck or chase a skater. A pack of dogs on the ice is a canine version of the Keystone Kops.

A thin skiff of snow over ice will give you traction if that snow has adhered to the ice surface; if not, it renders the ice all the more slippery. On sloping ice of the kind you might encounter on a sidewalk or unsanded city street, use the same shuffle step. In this situation it's critical, however, that you *keep your weight forward*. The natural tendency is to lean back while walking downhill on ice, but if you do, your feet will slip out from under you and you'll land — hard — on your rear end, or the back of your head.

Instead emulate the skier's crouch, leaning forward to keep your weight about mid-sole or toward the ball of your foot, but never on your heels. Shoulders are forward of hips, knees slightly bent. I taught this technique for walking down slippery slopes (it works on mud, too) to my father-in-law Rags Ragsdale, and now he calls it "the Groucho Marx walk." But forget Groucho's ramrod stiff back and ground-eating stride.

For steep icy slopes in the mountains, of course, you'll want to attach crampons to your boots, but in more moderately icy situations try "creepers." These are a kind of miniature version of a mountaineering crampon, available at sporting-goods or boot stores. A small plate of teethed metal, it attaches to the sole of your shoe or hiking boot with an elastic band. On winter jogs, I often encounter a woman who motors easily up and down the icy mountain trails above town on a pair of creepers, while I slip and slide and fall to my hands and knees whenever I attempt the same trails in my running shoes.

John Viehman straps on crampons before heading toward the 14,410-foot summit of Mount Rainier, Washington State.

Safety on Ice

Breaking through ice can be a life-threatening situation. Your sodden clothing increases your weight and restricts your mobility, and you have little point of purchase by which to pull yourself out. You are immersed in frigid water, giving you only a short time before fatal hypothermia sets in. In a wilderness setting, even if you are able to pull yourself out quickly, you still have the difficult task of warming yourself back to normal temperature — not easy if your spare clothing and sleeping bag are wet also, and you're unable to start a fire.

If you can possibly reroute your expedition to avoid ice of unknown thickness and configuration, do so. If not, there are several steps you can take to reduce the risk of outright disaster.

ICE-CROSSING PRECAUTIONS. Unless you are certain beyond doubt of an ice surface's integrity, never chance it if you are alone. If this means aborting your backcountry mission, so be it.

Even if you are with companions, equip yourself with a crossbeam to assist in self-rescue. This can be a ski, or a piece of driftwood left streamside by last spring's run-off; the latter will be dry and subject to fracture, so choose a stick at least 6 feet long and 6 inches in diameter. Carry your crossbeam laterally across your chest. Should you break through, it provides a support on which you can lever yourself up.

Snowshoes or skis increase your safety factor by more widely distributing your weight, but they are no panacea. Before setting out across the ice, loosen the bindings so you can kick them off if you do go down.

Any group anticipating ice crossings should carry rope and carabiners. One party member goes first, roped up under the arms. Once she makes it safely to the other side, the others should clip the carabiners to a sturdy belt loop or some other secure anchor point, thread the rope, and proceed in widely spaced single file. Meanwhile, the trail-blazer should have easily accessible a sleeping bag or spare set of clothing, against the chance of mishap. Anyone who is immersed for even a minute is likely to have onset symptoms of mild hypothermia (see page 190).

SELF-RESCUE. In the situation where you break through ice and must depend on yourself to get out, it's vital to note the fine line between adrenaline rush and panic. Stay on the former side of the line.

As you feel the ice give, throw your arms to either side to keep your head and upper torso above water. Take a deep breath, scissor-kick hard, and lunge forward, thrusting your arms ahead of you. When your hips are on solid ice, roll and continue to roll. Then slide across the ice on your stomach to shore.

It's possible the ice around you will be too thin for support. In that case, you'll have to break the ice with your fists or body until you reach stronger purchase. Work back in the direction from which you walked; you know that the ice is thicker in that direction.

Should all else fail, and if the day is very cold (at least zero), you might be able to gain leverage by allowing your gloves to freeze to the ice. Cramp your fingers so your hands don't slip free.

Self-rescue devices have up- and downsides. A pair of ice awls stowed where you can easily reach them helps give you purchase on the ice should you fall through. You can make a set yourself: Drill out one end of each of two 6-inch lengths of thick dowel, and insert thick-gauge nails. In the other ends, install screw-type rings and attach with rope so the device can be hung around the neck during dicey crossings. If you go in, you can theoretically pike yourself out.

The disadvantages are several. Any sharp implement, and any rope around your neck, is inherently dangerous; in the course of your plunge, you could stab or choke yourself, or

TECHNIQUE TIP

CREEK CROSSING

The staff at the Voyageur Outward Bound School in Ely, Minnesota, shared with us two hints on assessing the safety of a frozen-over stream. If it's covered with snow, check for grayish-colored bowl-like depressions; these indicate that water has seeped up through the ice into the snow. For bare ice, tap with a ski pole or stick; solid ice will return a reassuring tick, while thin or perched ice will sound hollow. "Perched" means there is air below the ice; lacking the support provided by resting on water, it is more likely to give way.

simply lose the gear. To bring it into play, you must sacrifice your spread-eagled, stabilized position. Still, if you do fall through, twin awls are better than nothing at all.

ASSISTED RESCUE. The essential item to have handy in an ice rescue is a length of good rope to throw to the victim. Other useful devices are the spare tire from a car, which can act as a lifebuoy; a ladder to slide across the ice and extend to the victim; or simply a long branch.

When no rope or device with reach is available, you as the rescuer must get within a few feet of the victim. The worst thing you can do is put yourself in unnecessary danger; accidents in which both victim and rescuer perish are tragically common.

Think of the rescue as having three stages, and rush none of them: You must reach the victim; you must pull the victim from the water; you must get the victim to safety.

Prepare for the second step before assaying the first: Look for anything that can serve as an impro-vised "rope." This can be a leather belt, heavyweight jacket (or several knotted together), backpack, sleeping bag, or dog leash. Ideally it should have the flexibility of these sorts of items, since the victim's ability to grip will be diminished by immer-sion. A basketed ski pole is better than nothing, though a snow-slicked deadwood stick may be useless.

Slide across the ice on your stomach to maximize the distribution of your weight. If possible, enhance this advantage by lying atop some-thing larger than you, such as two or more skis or a "raft" of long branches.

If other party members are pre-sent, they should form a human chain behind you, holding each other by the ankles, arms fully extended to increase as much as possible the dis-tance between each rescuer. This configuration also provides a belay against the weight of the victim as he climbs out of the water.

When alone, you should secure yourself to the ice somehow, against the chance of being dragged into the water as you try to pull the victim out. A pocket knife stabbed into the ice beats no belay at all.

Once out of the water, the victim likely will be hypothermic or pan-icked or both. Since one symptom of the former is irrationality, it's up to you to keep the victim calm. The rescue is not complete until the victim is dry, warm, and returned to normal body temperature. In the past, experts have suggested that rolling in snow will wick moisture from wet clothing. Although true, it will still leave the victim in frozen, snow-encrusted duds. The important thing is to get the victim into dry clothing and a warm place.

DRESSING FOR WINTER

A few days after completing my junior year of high school, I left the Midwest flatlands with two buddies for a hiking and skiing trip in Colorado. It was our first trip to the high country, and it failed to occur to us that June weather in the Rockies might vary just a tad from Wisconsin.

On the second day of our hike, we awoke before dawn at 12,000 feet with something cold and wet pressing against our smooth young faces. It was the fabric of our pup tent, which had collapsed under an overnight foot of new snow.

Our "expeditionary" clothing, chosen from the sweater-and-wind-breaker group, was just enough to warm us if we kept moving vigorously — which we did, downhill toward civilization. But my chums, apparently thinking of those barefoot June days in the Midwest, hadn't worn socks inside their hiking boots.

After an hour or two of tromping through the snow, they couldn't feel their feet. Presently they began to moan, and finally they couldn't walk any farther. We stopped, built a fire, and defrosted their feet. Ultimately we reached the car, but it had been a sobering experience for a group of kids on a lark.

We eventually learned to consider conditions and choose clothing to match. We've found that with the correct types and amounts of garb, there are almost no winter weather conditions in which you cannot be perfectly comfortable — and being comfortable is the single most important factor in winter pursuits. This book is about fun, and only a fool would engage in these activities if they meant misery.

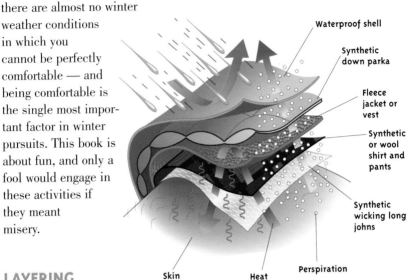

Layering in Winter

Waterproof shell

Synthetic down parka

Fleece jacket or vest

Synthetic or wool shirt and pants

Synthetic wicking long johns

Skin

Heat

Perspiration

LAYERING

Winter dressing is a matter of wearing layers, for several advantageous reasons. Layering allows you to increase or decrease the amount of clothing you have on to warm up or avoid overheating. It traps air inside your garments, turning them into an insulative ally instead of a cold-sucking enemy. It lets evaporation occur, and thus keeps the air inside

your clothing dry. Finally, layering captures and contains the heat that your body emits.

The Layers

No matter how many garments you wear, they fall into three categories. From inner to outer, they are:
● *The vapor layer*, which wicks body moisture away to keep you from becoming soaked next to the skin.
● *The insulative layer*, which warms by holding body-produced heat within your garment system.
● *The protective layer*, which is your "shell" or first defense against the elements. Its main purpose is to keep you dry.

THE VAPOR LAYER. The material for the vapor layer moves the perspira-

---

DID YOU KNOW

To reduce the scratchiness of wool garments next to the skin, add 1 tablespoon of olive oil per washload.

---

tion that you produce even at rest past its barrier, while at the same time contributing to the overall warmth of your layers. Under laboratory conditions, nothing fulfills these requirements better than wool. However, it is rarely used in practical situations because it does not resist wind well and is heavy, bulky and scratchy.

Today nearly all winter outdoorspersons have replaced wool with undergarments made of synthetic fabrics. Polypropylene is an efficient and relatively inexpensive choice, lightweight, pliant, and comfortable against the skin. Its disadvantage is that it does not preserve skin temperature, although the skin does not feel cold.

The state of the art is arguably Capilene. This synthetic is a weave of hollow microscopic fibers with a hydrophobic (moisture-hating) core, which repels water and sends it to the surface, and a hydrophilic (moisture-loving) exterior, which embraces and evaporates moisture, using body heat as an energy source.

We recommend Capilene for the sheath next to the skin. Balancing weight, cost, durability, breathability, and versatility, it is unbeatable. Capilene is produced in at least four weights, from a thin silk-like fabric to a fleece suitable for extreme outdoor conditions. Every type of undergarment is marketed in Capilene (see Patagonia, Sources & Resources), including long-sleeved T-shirts, tights, socks, and underwear for both men and women.

THE INSULATIVE LAYER. While the vapor layer is usually skintight, the insulative layer should be more loose-fitting. Again your object is to conserve body heat, and to allow moisture to vent.

Traditionally, the insulative layer was chosen from fleece or pile made from felt, but again synthetics have largely taken over the market. One of the best is Synchilla, a fleece that can be made from recycled plastic products (see "Fashion Alert," page 177). Polypropylene is another good choice. Avoid cotton, which retains

DID YOU KNOW

Shivering is one of the body's mechanisms for warming itself through extra exertion, but the goose bumps that often accompany it serve no purpose whatsoever — at least not at our present state of evolution. "Cutis anserine" (goose bumps) is caused by contraction of the arrectores pilorum, minute erector muscles at the base of body hair. It is a throwback to the time of our fur-bearing ancestors and their ability to fluff up their pelts in the cold to make a thicker, more air-entrapping coat.

moisture and wicks it poorly.

THE PROTEC-TIVE LAYER. Outer jackets and leggings fall into two types: shells, and insulated jackets, parkas, or leggings. In either case, they ideally allow body-produced moisture to continue on its way to the general atmosphere, while keeping rain or snowmelt from penetrating.

Shells are unlined, like the "windbreaker" of your youth. Unfortunately, that now-outdated garment only did the second part of the job, expelling external wetness while trapping perspiration. The solution came in 1975 with the introduction of Gore-Tex, a sort of clothing equivalent of the one-way valve. Gore-Tex is a laminate bonded to polyester or nylon and containing microscopic pores too small to admit water in liquid form, yet large enough to allow water vapor to escape, a quality known as "breathability."

A protective layer that is lined incorporates aspects of the insulative layer; depending on your needs, it can either augment or replace the latter. The lining may be a solid fabric such as fleece, felt, or

How Gore-Tex Works

The microscopic holes in the Gore-Tex laminate allow tiny perspiration droplets to escape, yet are so small they keep raindrops out.

Polyester or nylon shell

Gore-Tex laminate

Lining

polypropylene, or a quilting filled with air-dependent insulation, either synthetic or natural.

The latter is one of the few clothing ingredients in which nature has not yet been overwhelmingly supplanted by human-made substances. All major outlets continue to offer jackets containing goose down, the least bulky and warmest filling when encased in a waterproof fabric. Down in a nylon liner also has a "warm" feel against your skin that on a cold night adds immeasurably to its appeal.

However, the key here is "waterproof"; when wet, down clumps, thereby reducing air space and warmth. In practice, you're unlikely to encounter absolutely dry conditions in the field, and for that reason down, despite its advantages, is going the way of other natural materials, especially now that advances in synthetics are decreasing their bulk.

These polyester microfibers are

engineered to mimic down's advantages. Their ability to trap air when wet is impressive; they possess plasticity, the property of springing back; and they are inarguably warm. Among the proprietary fillings with these properties are Primaloft, Polargard, Quallofil, and Hollofil II.

BOOTS

The perfect boot has an upper that is well insulated for warmth and firm for ankle support, yet is lightweight and flexible for striding comfort. Its sole is deeply ridged for traction and rigid enough to take a crampon, but doesn't have a "tippy" feeling when you're on ice or bare ground. The sole bends easily in a Telemark binding, while the toe is reinforced for kick-stepping and sled-braking but does not confine your toes.

In other words, the perfect boot does not and probably cannot exist. Your choice is dictated by your pro-

FASHION ALERT

A major new approach in clothing production has received a strongly positive response from both consumers and environmentalists. Increasingly, materials from fleece to "cotton" are spun from recycled plastic and are going into sweaters, pants, underwear, T-shirts, and virtually every other type of garment. Nine billion bottles for beverages and grocery items are produced in this country annually from a plastic called polyethylene terephthalate, or PET. While two-thirds of the non-biodegradable empties end up in landfills, over 7,000 community curbside recycling programs are channeling the rest to firms like Wellman, Inc., a Fortune 500 company in Bridgeport, New Jersey.

Wellman handles more than $2^1/2$ billion PET bottles each year, yet demand still outstrips supply. To process the bottles, they are sorted by color, cleaned, and chopped into flakes. These are melted and spun into fibers thinner than a human hair.

Patagonia and Moving Comfort are among the several dozen clothing manufacturers that have incorporated PET-based clothing into their lines, and the New Hampshire-based retail chain Eastern Mountain Sports reports that PET dominates their sales of fleece garments. How do they feel and perform? For warmth, comfort, and durability, it's difficult to tell the difference between PET and polyester, and for quick drying PET is a bit superior.

The well-dressed winter traveler. An outer waterproof protective jacket with attached hood, sunglasses, insulated gloves, and gaiters to keep snow from entering at boot-tops all contribute to safe, comfortable winter adventures.

posed activity, and as you expand your winter adventure horizons, you'll find the floor of your closet taken up by an increasing inventory of more specialized footwear.

In every case, however, your selection will be based on five factors, all of them involving trade-offs.

Waterproofing

It is absolutely essential that your feet remain dry. Wet feet are uncomfortable at best, dangerous at worst; in extreme conditions, you are exposing yourself to frostbite.

Impermeability is a function of the outer material, which can be rubber or pre-treated leather (avoid leather/nylon combinations; these are summer models). Rubber is absolutely waterproof and signifi-

cantly less expensive, but also less durable, less warm, and will trap perspiration within.

Quality leather boots are pre-treated for waterproofing, but should be re-treated periodically after use. Follow the manufacturer's or retailer's or recommendation in choosing a treatment that is effective without compromising the material's breathability.

No matter how waterproof the outer material, it won't help if snow seeps into the boot top. Rubber boots call for gaiters (see page 180) if you anticipate deep snow. Most leather models feature a rubber-encased foam collar that fits snugly around the leg and goes a long way toward obviating the problem, but gaiters are still recommended.

Warmth

There's a reason the term "cold feet" is slang for lack of courage: Chilled digits have been the reason for aborting too many trips.

Rubber or leather is too thin to provide much insulation by itself, so all winter boots require a lining. The warmest is polyester fleece or felt, which is usually found in rubber boots, or "pacs" (some models have leather uppers — the part above the ankle — and rubber lowers). Felt or fleece, however, is usually in the form of an insert that is not bonded to the outer material, and it makes for a loose fit and less comfort when walking. Felt also compresses over time and becomes less insulative.

A sewn-in layer of a synthetic, most often Thinsulate and available only in a leather boot, is lighter, thinner, and more comfortable. An inner lining of proprietary fabric such as Gore-Tex or Cambrelle helps wick perspiration.

In earlier days, Native Americans who wore boots of sealskins packed the footbeds with dried grass. We bring this up as a reminder that you must have insulation not only beside the foot, but underfoot as well, where the most cold-inducing contact takes place. Insulative padding, lined in polypropylene or nylon, not only provides another layer of warmth between you and the snow, but makes for less jarring walking. It's especially important with stiff soles, which by themselves

are comparatively colder, since you produce less muscle warmth through foot flexing.

Comfort

The folk wisdom "When your feet hurt, you hurt all over" also has merit. The key to comfort is fit, which should be approached as a way to solve the "hug/snug" paradox.

Even a top-notch rubber boot cannot be designed to hug the foot,

DID YOU KNOW

Women who report that they get cold outdoors more easily than men have science to back their claim. While women may carry an extra layer of body fat that helps insulate them against the cold, they also possess less muscle in proportion to their body surface area than men, according to Women's Sports and Fitness magazine. This means that they can't generate as much heat from muscle activity as men. One key to staying warm for women is to maintain an adequate iron supply in their diet; studies have shown that women with low-iron blood have difficulty regulating and retaining body heat.

and therein lies a pitfall. Annoying slippage as you walk may tempt you to purchase a smaller size; the penalty for this mistake is cramped toes that limit both the distance you can cover and the enjoyment therein. Worst, you'll quickly wear out the insulation at the toes, and tight fit combined with thin cover is an invitation to frostbite.

Leather boots are more "shoe-like," and can be much more closely fitted to the contour of individual feet. If you have even moderate ambitions of perambulating in the winter outdoors, they are well worth the additional investment.

Weight

Manufacturers generally classify their various models as lightweight, mid-weight, and expedition-weight (for obvious marketing reasons, no boot-maker wants to use the term "heavy-weight"). For winter wear, your leather boot will run in the latter two categories. A general-purpose pair will weigh between 3 and 4 pounds (or up to 5 pounds and a few ounces

for mountaineering). Though not an insignificant burden, it's one you will wish to bear in exchange for warmth and general-purpose durability.

Sole

Golf cleats enhance your traction as you take your stance to tee off, but are definitely problematic if you are negotiating a polished ballroom floor. Similarly, the tread of a winter boot must suit the terrain you are crossing. A deep-cut, toothed configuration will take you up a steep slope of dense snow, but the lightly ribbed rubber sole of a pac grips with more traction on flat ice.

The second consideration in a sole, stiffness, also must fit the purpose to which it is put. The thickest, most rigid soles incorporate embedded steel shanks; they take a crampon and support you when you kick in, but range from uncomfortable to painful for walking on the flat. In all but extreme conditions, choose a sole that at least compromises with your foot's desire to flex at the ball and ankle as you stride.

GEAR TALK

GAITERS

Gaiters are "chaps" of a sort, tubes usually of treated nylon that encase the legs below the knee and flare over your boots to prevent loose snow from sifting inside the tops. Gaiters also keep your trouser bottoms dry, and some are lined for extra warmth. Whether you plan to walk, ski, or snow-shoe, gaiters are an inexpensive and utilitarian addition to your wardrobe.

SOCKS

Like all vapor layers, socks should be of material that is warm when damp yet wicks that dampness away from your skin. Wool qualifies on the first count, and in a sock its itchiness can be avoided by wearing it over a thin inner sock usually made from a synthetic such as Capilene. Note that most socks, outer and inner, are actually hybrids. In referring to wool, we include combinations such as 80 percent wool with nylon and a touch of Lycra for stretchability; similarly, in most Capilene liners, other materials are often present.

Even at high altitudes, when carrying heavy loads on bright, calm days there will be times when you will want to shed certain layers. Most people begin by removing their hat or unzipping their outer jacket.

Decide on your socks before shopping for a pair of boots, and remember to wear or bring them to the store for purposes of fitting.

HANDS

The choice between gloves and mittens is frequently couched in terms of a great debate. It should not be. Its essence is simply a trade-off between dexterity and warmth, and depends on what activities you plan to pursue.

Mittens keep your hands warmer because they place less of your skin area near the cold air. They are also clumsily difficult to manipulate; while mittens are adequate for gripping the steering bar of

A thin fleece liner mitten (right) topped by a waterproof shell (left) are the keys to warm hands.

IS IT FOGGY OR IS THAT JUST ME?

Especially when you are breathing hard or the day is gray and moist, condensation on the lenses of your glasses or goggles is a likely, and irritating, event.

Defoggers are of two types. Treated polishing cloths do the job but have to be frequently reapplied, an inconvenience in the field. We prefer one of the commercial substances that is rubbed on the lenses prior to setting out; their ingredients are typically

detergent, glycerine, and a base such as vegetable oil, mixed to a waxy consistency. Expect to pay about $8 an ounce, but that quantity provides at least 50 applications. For a less expensive alternative, experiment with various plain shampoos; several of the athletes we met while luging at Lake Placid used a brand called "Body on Tap."

Incidentally, our banker uses wax defogger on his computer screen. In addition to preventing condensation, this type also repels lint and dust.

a Flexible Flyer, they come up short when you are trying to shoot a photograph or dice the vegetables for a winter-campsite stew.

The solution is to wear mittens for warmth and gloves for dexterity. In other words, layer your hands much as you'll layer your torso, removing or adding layers according to use requirements and cold conditions.

The inner layer consists of a thin liner glove of silk or polypropylene. The insulative layer is either a wool or synthetic glove, and the shell layer is a waterproof mitten large enough to fit over the other two. Of course, only in more extreme conditions will you need all three layers.

ABOVE THE NECK

Mission Control for overall body temperature is located topside, specifically in the region of the hypothalamus at the base of the brain. There receptors monitor blood temperature, as well as data called in from nerves located in your skin that act much like thermostats in the rooms of a house.

The skull surrounding this main sensor is thin and covered with little body fat, and the vessels in the neck that feed blood to it are close to the skin surface where they are easily chilled by cold air. More than a tenth of the heat that your body radiates comes from topside. This is why it's so important to wear a hat in winter, but what's surprising is how many people don't and then complain that they are cold.

Depending on conditions, add a scarf or a dickey to protect your neck. And make sure your parka is zipped to your chin.

Better still, choose a parka with a

windproof hood as an adjunct to your hat and neck warmer. While cruising through an iceberg-clogged sea in small outboard boats with the Inuit of northern Greenland, we noted that they were perfectly comfortable in thin, white anoraks while we were shivering despite our heavy coats. Aside from the fact that the natives were accustomed to the cold more than we, their anoraks were hand-sewn with carefully fitted hoods that not only sealed the warm air in and prevented it from escaping through their collars, but, just as important, covered every square inch of their necks.

In extreme conditions, consider replacing the plain hat with a face mask, or balaclava. This is a hood of wool or synthetic that pulls down over the entire face, with gaps for the eyes and, ideally, for the mouth, so water vapor can be expelled.

When facing frigid winds, a soft, synthetic fleece balaclava worn under a hat or hood provides superb warmth and protection to the face.

Eye Protection

Our friend Skip Horner, the first professional guide to place clients on each of the highest summits on the seven continents, tells of a party member who was forced to stay behind at High Camp on Mount Everest while Skip successfully guided the rest of his group to the summit. The unfortunate climber was a victim of snow blindness; the previous day he had rejected Skip's advice to dig his sunglasses out of his pack.

For more on this condition and its treatment, see page 192. Its cause is bright sunshine reflecting off snow, especially in concave bowls. Snow blindness can occur at any elevation, although it is more common at higher altitudes, where the sun's rays are filtered through less of the earth's atmosphere.

Prevention is elementary: wear goggles or sunglasses with lenses that block at least 90 percent of ultraviolet radiation. Almost all commercial and prescription sunglasses meet this standard, but for safety's sake, check with your retailer or ophthalmologist. Choose lenses that are large and curved, or a frame equipped with side and top covers to stop light from those directions.

In an emergency, you can improvise eye protection. Cut a piece of cardboard or whatever material is available into eyeglass shape, and make a thin slit or pinpoint in it. Your field of vision will be reduced, but your eyes will be protected. This slit-type goggle was the "sunglass" that Inuits tra-ditionally fashioned from a piece of hide or bone to protect themselves against the dazzling brightness of the Arctic summer.

Mountaineering sunglasses feature full ultraviolet protection, removable leather side shields, and replaceable parts. Where painful snow blindness is a danger, such shades are far more than a fashion statement.

SKIN PROTECTION

The two main threats to skin are dry-ness and sunburn.

Petroleum jelly remains the single best defense against dryness. It "waterproofs" the skin, keeping natural moisture where it belongs while also serving as a layer of pro-tection against wind. A bit of grease also feels good to most people, but if you are not among them, a lotion or cream will also do the job. Both Noxema and Nutragena offer a variety of appropriate applications.

From a purely pragmatic point of view, the best way to prevent sunburn is by building up a natural tan through repeated short periods of

The right clothing is just as important at the neighborhood sledding hill as on a mountainside, especially where a child's enthusiasm holds sway over common sense.

of skin.

Sunblocks provide a barrier that completely shuts out ultraviolet radiation. Most contain an opaque pigment such as zinc oxide or titanium dioxide. Complete blocking is not usually necessary, but you might wish it if you are fair-skinned or you expect to be on snow in bright sunshine at high altitude.

exposure. However, you are not likely to be very bronzed in the middle of winter and you may not care to be, since tanning has been implicated in skin cancer.

The alternative is a sunscreen or sunblock. *Sunscreens* are rated according to their "Sun Protection Factor." The SPF is a multiplier of the amount of time a user of a given lotion would become sunburned without any protection at all. In other words, if under given conditions your skin would begin to redden in 30 minutes, a sunscreen with an SPF of 10 will ward off burn for 5 hours.

The most common screening ingredient is para-aminobenzoic acid. PABA may cause dermatitis, an irritating if temporary inflammation of the skin; it's most likely in younger children. Before deciding to take a product into the field, each person who will be using it should test it on a small patch

Three precautions should be kept in mind. First, make sure all exposed skin is covered, including lips and any part of the ears not covered by your hat. We're particularly prone to getting sunburned on our earlobes and have learned not to miss that spot with the lotion.

Second, remember that all sun preparations can be diluted or washed off by perspiration or inadvertently wiped away. Frequent reapplication is a wise idea.

Last, note that one can't see one's own face. Keep an eye on your companions for signs of reddening.

CHOOSING CLOTHING FOR THE CONDITIONS

A layering system allows you to

adjust your clothing by removing or adding a layer to adjust to changing conditions and changes in the degree to which you're exerting yourself. Sometimes, however, it's difficult to know what layers to choose in the first place. When dressing for an outing, consider three variables:

WEATHER. Conditions outdoors in the winter, as we have emphasized throughout this book, are infinitely variable. Temperatures rise or fall precipitously over a very short period. Snow squalls appear from sky that was clear an hour earlier. A 15-degree day with sunshine reflected from the snow feels like 40 degrees; a front passes, a 10-mile-per-hour wind comes up, and now it feels like 3 degrees, or even colder. When the sun drops below the horizon, the temperature suddenly plummets 20 degrees.

TERRAIN. In mountains, as a rule of thumb, the temperature drops 3 to 5 degrees for every 1,000 vertical feet. But altitude is not the only topological factor to consider. You may experience either colder or warmer air near large bodies of water if there is a large temperature difference either way between the lake and the air. Wind velocity, which plays an enormous role in determining how cold it feels and how you should dress, is a function of your position. On exposed ridges or open plains, you have to plan on carrying windproof clothing; down in sheltered valleys or forests, it's less of a consideration.

ACTIVITY. The more vigorous the activity, the more heat you'll generate, and the less clothing you'll need. Of course, if you plan to remain outdoors after you stop that vigorous activity, you'll want extra layers.

Here is where the sweat/shiver paradox rears its confounding head.

DID YOU KNOW
The traditional cold-weather clothing for the world's farthest-north people, the Inuit of northern Greenland, is a pair of polar-bear pants, a coat of fox fur, and mittens of seal or caribou skin, writes Peter Freuchen in his *Book of the Eskimos*. Footwear consists of a pair of sealskin boots that have been packed with dried grass to provide an insulating cushion under the sole. The Inuit wear their outer garments fairly loosely to vent perspiration, except for a closely-fitting bird skin shirt they wear underneath with its feathers against their skin. Using thread made of narwhal sinew, the Inuit women stitch together these elaborate outfits with such care, writes Freuchen, that it "puts the finest Paris furrier to shame."

Even moderate exercise will produce perspiration, and no matter how efficient your layering system, you're going to be wet on the inside on some treks. This goes from being inconvenient to being darned uncomfortable, or even dangerous, if there isn't a hot shower at your destination. In winter camping at the end of a long hike or ski, for example, your level of activity as you set up your gear is less than when you were moving along. It is also later in the day and growing colder, and you'll very soon start to shiver.

The solution is to get into dry clothing as quickly as possible. If you are building a fire, do so first thing. Otherwise, erect your shelter, get inside, change your vapor layer, and only then see to the remaining chores. The sweat/shiver syndrome occurs even during simple day outings.

On Telemark ski outings, one friend of ours sweats his way to the top of the slope and, though the air temperature might hover around zero, surprises his companions by stripping to the waist. He then takes a fresh, dry jersey from the top of his pack, pulls it overhead, adds a pile jacket and parka, and, warm and comfortable, is ready for a picnic lunch in the snow before a run through the powder to the bottom.

Alternatives and Modifications to Layering

For shorter day-trip activities, it may be appropriate to decide in advance to neglect layering adjustments. If you're taking part in particularly vigorous exercise that is sure to warm you quickly — a snowshoe race, for example — you may choose to "start out cold."

This is safe and suitable only if the degree of discomfort is moderate, its period brief, and once you warm up you expect to maintain a pace that will warm you soon after starting out and keep you warm until your return to the indoors. If you plan to stop for a half-hour picnic at the top of that 7,000-foot mountain, you'll definitely want the extra jersey. Even without any mid-trip pause, you'll still carry that jersey if there is any chance of the weather changing for the worse. If you don't otherwise need a pack, you can tie the garment around your waist by the sleeves when it is not needed.

If you don't mind a little extra exercise, it's possible to use the start-out-cold approach without actually being cold at all. Ten minutes of aerobic indoor warm-up will prepare your body. Don't work out to the point of breaking a sweat, and dress and get outdoors immediately afterward. Alternatively, you might wear an extra layer for the first leg of the trip and then doff and stash it trailside if your return route is the same.

In every case, the bottom-line rule in dressing for winter is to err on the side of caution and warmth.

SAFETY IN
THE WINTER
OUTDOORS

W hen you sit around and address the issue of winter back-country safety — as we did the other day — Jack London invariably comes up. Who among us can avoid the lit-eral frisson produced when reading his chilling short story "To Build a Fire," in which a solo dogsledder becomes wet when he breaks through ice over a creek on a 50-below Yukon day and. . .well, let's not ruin the grisly ending for those few who didn't read this tale in junior high.

London's story is so compelling because we naturally consider cold to be a threat to health and well-being. This is not entirely rational; extreme heat is equally dangerous, yet cold seems to be a more psychologically vivid ogre. If you've ever read a detailed account of someone dying of thirst and heat in a desert, you'll vastly prefer extreme cold.

MEDICAL EMERGENCIES
A degree of risk is inherent whenever you venture into the backcountry, and cold can magnify the subsequent peril you face. Prevention is, as the adage has it, the superior of the cure — but when accidents do happen, knowledge and the right gear are your keys to helping yourself and keeping the situation from getting worse.

Note that with any serious injury or condition, evacuation to a medical facility is the best course, although evacuation can be made more difficult by severe cold or deep snows. Evacuation may require a wait or be unavailable, in which case you must take certain steps to alleviate the situation. Nonetheless, the interventional first aid suggested here should always be followed up by professional medical attention on your return to civilization.

Hypothermia

Hypothermia is a reduction in the temperature of the body's core. Although exposure and cold temperature (although not necessarily that cold; hypothermia can occur when it is as warm as 55 degrees) are its primary causes, your susceptibility increases through inadequate intake of calories and fluid; inadequate sobriety; and, as physician and wilderness medicine expert James Wilkerson points out (see Sources & Resources), "inadequate money for housing, heat, clothing, and food." Wilkerson writes that, statistically, hypothermia is more common in an urban environment than in the wilderness.

Hypothermia may be diagnosed as mild or severe; the former invariably precedes the latter. Its signs and symptoms are blue lips; shivering that you cannot control through force

CHILLING OUT

The Antarctic cod is unconcerned about hypothermia, even though the seawater off the coast of the southernmost continent stands at 28.6 degrees year-round. The cod has evolved an intriguing countermeasure: the ability to manufacture its own antifreeze.

Unlike the ethylene glycol in your auto's radiator, which chemically lowers the freezing point, the peptides and glycopeptides produced in the liver of Dissostichus mawsoni alter the water's physics. "The fish breathes ice crystals, which normally want to grow," says Charles Knight, senior scientist at the National Center for Atmospheric Research in Boulder, Colorado. "This makes them not want to grow."

Knight and other researchers have bioengineered one-celled organisms that produce the same substances. In the future, they hope to derive methods of synthesizing them in quantity, for potential applications ranging from increasing the longevity and palatability of frozen foods to preservation of human blood and donor organs during transport.

High wind and snow; ascent of Mount Rainier, Washington State. Under these conditions the onset of hypothermia or frostbite can be very rapid. Eating and drinking regularly to maintain heat production and dressing properly are vital to healthy, safe outings.

of will; fatigue; loss of coordination; and uncharacteristic irritability. Wilkerson advises that you observe a potential victim for the "umbles": He mumbles, fumbles, stumbles, tumbles, and grumbles.

Treat mild hypothermia by warming: Remove wet clothing, put on extra layers of dry clothes, expose the victim to an open fire, and walk him around to generate heat by exercising large muscles. Until fairly recently, it was recommended that the victim be undressed and placed in a sleeping bag with another person, but this is now discouraged. It is possible that blood has pooled in the muscles and become acidic, and if warmed too quickly by skin-to-skin contact, can return to the heart and cause shock or cardiac arrest.

Severe hypothermia, defined as a core body temperature below 90 degrees, is a medical emergency. Wilkerson writes frankly and vividly of the hopelessness of this situation when professional skills and equipment are far distant. His advice is unequivocal and incontrovertible: Observe yourself and your fellow party members for mild hypothermia, and treat it before it progresses.

Frostbite

Frostbite is the freezing of tissue. It most commonly affects body parts that expose the greatest area of skin to cold, such as fingers, toes, nose, and earlobes. Less often seen, but still of concern, are cheeks and the corneas of the eyes; the latter can become frostbitten when a snowmobile is driven at high speed and the driver is not protected by goggles. Constrictive clothing that is not adequately insulated, such as thin boots or gloves, also encourages frostbite.

The mild onset stage, sometimes called frostnip or superficial frostbite, is characterized by whitening of the skin and numbness. The skin, however, remains soft. Rewarm frostnip using skin-to-skin contact. Never massage, rub with snow, or use an external heat source. Warm frostnipped hands by placing your bare hands inside your vapor layer and under your armpits; for feet, the best body-heat source is a companion's stomach. Take special care to avoid refreezing; tissue that thaws and refreezes suffers significantly greater damage.

True, or deep, frostbite is indicated when the skin is numb, cold, white, and rock hard. DO NOT rewarm in the field. Once thawed, the area is useless and excruciatingly painful. Deep frostbite requires evacuation. Improper thawing can lead to infection and amputation.

Snow Blindness

The prevention of snow blindness is discussed in Chapter 13. It is not uncommon among those who visit the high mountains for the first time and don't take adequate measures to prevent it. Its cause is absorption by the surface of the eye — the cornea and conjunctiva — of ultraviolet radiation. In other words, these tissues can be sunburned just as the skin can.

Snow blindness is insidious in that you have no sensation of its onslaught, aside from possibly noting that sunlight appears especially bright. The palpable symptoms of photophthalmia, as it's known medically, will generally not appear for 8 to 12 hours. They include dryness and irritation which progresses to extreme pain. Blinking the eyelids or moving the eyeballs may convince you that your orbs are drenched in grating sand.

Most commonly, snow blindness will heal itself in a few days. Ulceration of the cornea, producing permanent damage, is possible but less likely. The treatment is darkness, cool compresses, and time; aspirin should help reduce the torment.

As with so many winter calamities, prevention is the best route. We always pack a pair of goggles or sunglasses, no matter what the weather or season, if we plan to be anywhere near snow. On a 4-day June hike into the Bitterroot Mountains, the two of us had to cross several large snowfields on a sunny day. We carried only a single pair of sunglasses, and had to trade them off among the leader, with the person in front wearing the sunglasses and the other holding his hand, groping blindly along with eyes closed.

Trauma

While both you and the landscape are well padded with clothing and mounds of snow during the winter, traumatic accidents can and do occur. Most common are cuts, sprains, and fractured limbs. The last — and the first two as well if they are serious — demands professional treatment as soon as available, but until then, first aid will assist eventual recovery.

Two errors are made with unfortunate frequency in attention to *cuts* deep enough to produce significant bleeding. First, do *not* apply a tourniquet above the wound; the resulting cutoff of blood circulation puts the rest of the limb at risk of sacrifice. Instead, control the bleeding by direct pressure.

Second, resist the urge to close the wound. Doing so can seal in infection. Instead, irrigate with preboiled water and observe for redness or inflammation, which indicates infection's onslaught. In its absence after several days, the wound may be closed with a butterfly bandage or tape. Even many physicians do not suture wounds in the wilderness, because sterility is almost impossible to maintain.

Do not hike over snow without bringing along sunglasses, preferably ones like these, specially designed for the purpose. They include full ultraviolet protection and leather side shields.

A *sprain* occurs when the ligaments of a joint are either stretched or torn. In the former case, the sprain is mild, and the treatment mnemonic is ICE: Apply Ice, or cold, wrapping it in a cloth and examining the area frequently to avoid frostbite. Provide

DID YOU KNOW

In otherwise healthy and fit men and women, a cold rarely progresses to the point of medical emergency, but its symptoms can be a distinct irritation. To treat them, don't neglect that age-old palliative, a nice hot bowl of chicken soup.

According to Irwin Ziment of the UCLA School of Medicine, cooked chicken releases cystine, an amino acid similar to acetylcysteine, a medication routinely prescribed to thin mucus and originally extracted from chicken feathers and skin. Add carrots, onions, parsley, and celery for vitamin A, niacin, and riboflavin, and as much hot stuff — garlic, curry powder, spices — as you can handle, since they act as expectorants. Then dig in; as Mom always told me, "Eat, eat, life is short."

mild Compression, in the form of an elastic bandage or similar wrap, and Elevate the extremity.

Sprains involving torn ligaments are treated similarly to *fractures*, and ultimately demand evacuation. Until it arrives, immobilize the limb by splinting it with branches, skis, or ski poles; in the absence of rope or straps, the splint can be tied in place with socks or strips torn from clothing.

Whenever a victim is not ambulatory, he should be given liquids whether or not he professes thirst, and kept warmed and calmed. Maintain a cool head yourself as well; remember that you are not the person who is hurt, and that the one who is needs your moral support.

If self-evacuation is necessary, you'll need to improvise a litter. Consider all available material — that which you are carrying and that which nature offers. A travois can be built of deadfall boughs, a blanket, or a half-dozen skis lashed together, among other material. Take turns towing, and proceed deliberately; a simple fracture is rarely a medical emergency in itself but can become one with sufficient jostling of the victim.

NAVIGATION

We've often speculated how early explorers navigated in the absence of maps. How did Lewis and Clark, for instance, find their way from St.

A snowshoer in northern Utah's Wasatch Mountains pauses to consult his topographic map. Do not head off on the trail without one.

Louis to the Pacific without a Rand McNally tucked into their packs? The answer is that while they used compass and sextant, they mostly asked Indians, "Which way is the ocean?" On one occasion when local inquiry was unavailable, they took a wrong turn not far from where we live. Their misstep is memorialized in the name of a mountain crossing now easily traversed by U.S. Highway 12, but still known as "Lost Trail Pass."

You too can enter territory that is new to you without a map, and no matter how confident you are of your orienteering ability, you should be prepared to get lost. Too often that landmark another skier has told you that you "can't miss" turns out to be highly missable indeed. Information posted at a trailhead can be incomplete or erroneous. Elevated features may be higher, steeper, and farther away than they appear, especially against a flat winter sky.

Maps, and Reading Them

Possibly the most helpful charts are $7^{1}/_{2}$-minute topological (or "topo") maps, from the U.S. Geological Survey (see Sources & Resources). These have a generous scale of $2^{5}/_{8}$ inches to the mile, and each covers an area of about 6 by 9 miles. They include natural features such as forest, open ground, rivers, and lakes as well as human-made particulars including roads, buildings, powerlines, railroad tracks, and trails.

One extremely useful aspect of

It takes practice to read a map. Become familiar with maps by using them on dayhikes along well-marked trails so that when you need one, you'll have the skill to make good use of it. Arriving at a consensus is a good way to minimize error.

topological maps are the isobars indicating altitude above sea level. Again, the scale is large: Each bar denotes a rise of 40 feet. Heavier bars, 200 feet of altitude apart, are labeled with the elevation.

On any extended backcountry expedition, we like to take along both a 7½-minute map and a map that covers a wider stretch of terrain, so we know where we are in relation to major rivers, highways, towns, and the like. In our area, which is largely national forest, the latter maps are published by the U.S. Forest Service and show the entirety of whatever national forest we happen to be visiting that trip.

Study your route before leaving the comfort of home. Note any stream crossings and give particular attention to the spacing of the isobars. The closer they are, the steeper the terrain. For example, assume you count 25 bars (a 1,000-foot rise) in a half mile (2,640 feet). The steepness, determined by dividing 1000 by 2640, is expressed either as 38 percent or as 34 degrees (to convert percent to degrees, multiply by 0.9). This may sound moderate, but in fact it approaches the upper edge of what is climbable (or descendable) on snow without technical skills and equipment.

Two warnings about topological maps are in order. First, they are not always up-to-date, and both terrain and artificial features change. Clear-cuts become young forests and rivers cut new channels. Irrigation ditches are filled in, powerlines are replaced by underground cable, railroad tracks are torn up, broadcasting antennae are dismantled.

Worse, trails and logging roads can evaporate. A few years back, we embarked on a ski trip projected at 2 hours, based on the topo. We left one trail to bushwhack down to another — and found it completely overgrown with nearly impenetrable thicket at the base of a canyon bounded by cliffs and steep scree. It took us 10 hours to cover 3 miles, and we arrived at the car cold, exhausted, and badly dehydrated.

The date when a topo was surveyed, along with the date of any revisions, appears in the lower left corner. Check it before you risk your comfort and safety on the map's reliability.

Second, matching the actual topography to its map depiction requires skill and experience. It's a bit like learning a new alphabet to be able to "read" where the terrain dips and where it rises. It's easily misinterpreted, because there is a tendency to alter the map's topography to match how far along you wish you were, rather than how far along you actually are.

We have gone miles up the wrong trail, convincing ourselves periodically that the lakes we passed were "that one and that one and that

one" on the map. We've also climbed the wrong mountain, although we felt less bad about that goof when we heard from Skip Horner the story of his first attempt on Mount Vinson, the highest peak in Antarctica. With a group of clients who were paying dearly for the privilege, Skip got to the top — where, across a long ridge, they could see a summit that was obviously 50 feet higher. (Incidentally, Skip did guide them to the correct summit the next day.)

Using a Compass

A compass is a great aid in avoiding these kinds of mistakes, if you take the time to learn to use it. A compass has three parts: the flat base, also called the protractor; the dial, which revolves on the base; and the needle. An arrow is etched into the base, pointing from the dial to the top.

It is important to remember that the needle does not point to "true" north, the line from you to the geographical North Pole (see page 202). Instead the compass points to magnetic north. At the base of the topo map, you'll find a V-shaped graphic that indicates the declination, or difference, for your location.

To use the twin tools of map and compass to pinpoint your location, first *orient* the map. Place it on a flat surface, check your compass, and turn the map so its top is facing the direction the needle indicates. Now adjust for declination.

Next, find a landmark a couple

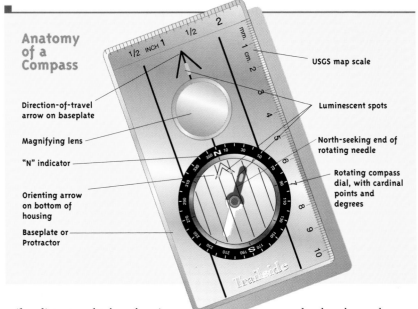

Anatomy of a Compass

Direction-of-travel arrow on baseplate

Magnifying lens

"N" indicator

Orienting arrow on bottom of housing

Baseplate or Protractor

USGS map scale

Luminescent spots

North-seeking end of rotating needle

Rotating compass dial, with cardinal points and degrees

miles distant and take a bearing on it (that is, point the compass arrow at it). Rotate the dial so the needle is aligned with north on the dial. If you are looking at the landmark you think you chose on the map, the needle points to the map's top. Keeping the needle so aligned, move the protractor so one upper corner is on the landmark and with a pencil draw a line along the edge.

Now find a second landmark in a different direction. Repeat the steps to draw a second line. The point on the map where the two lines cross marks "You Are Here."

If for some reason you are not carrying a compass, the map by itself can still give you information, albeit rougher, on where you are — but only if you can positively identify features. In that case, line up the map so it is in the same aspect as the

landmarks, and you can make a decent approximation of your location.

Getting Unlost

If you're like us, your first emotion upon getting lost will be denial. We bark, "I'm not lost, the map is wrong. That mountain should be over here. Any fool can see that's Flat-Top Butte."

When you finally accept that you are well and truly lost, it is a bewildering, frustrating, and infuriating experience. You may feel anger, helplessness, or panic. When we get lost, as we do with embarrassing frequency, though mostly on a minor scale, we still must fight the urge to thrash through the woods in search of the missing trail, a landmark, anything familiar.

When you feel that urge, counteract it by sitting down and calmly analyzing your situation. The first decision is whether to move or stay put.

If it is late in the day, you should almost always hold your position. Route finding after dark is difficult and dangerous; you can veer in the wrong direction, move in circles, or injure yourself or other party members in a fall. Even in daylight, consider remaining where you are if the weather is bad or threatens to turn bad, or if any of your group is at the point of fatigue.

A friend who writes on the outdoors — yes, there's some irony in this story — became if not utterly lost at least a long way from where he wanted to be. Evening approached, and he found himself thrashing through the underbrush in a tight drainage in an attempt to get to a road. He began to shake and tremble, and knew he was becoming hypothermic.

Wisely, he decided to give up the attempt for the night, and holed up under the big boughs of an old Douglas fir. He built a fire, melted some snow and rehydrated, and remained warm and dry until morning. He skied out of the woods just as the search-and-rescue helicopter was about to lift off from the airport.

MOVING OUT. If you do choose to try to find your way out, there are a few things you can do to maximize success, though none is without pitfalls.

The traditional advice of heading downhill or downstream has some

validity. However, the journey might be a long one and lead to further impediment. Logging roads in the

DID YOU KNOW

In Barrow, Alaska, the northernmost community in the United States, the sun dips below the horizon at 1:42 P.M. on the 18th of November and lies doggo until the 22nd of January, 65 days later. This got us wondering about the truth of a common wisdom, so we rang up the U.S. Naval Observatory to ask whether the North Pole really enjoys 6 months each of night and day.

The answer is yes, but only in theory. The sun does rise only once a year, but nuances of twilight and the planet's imperfectly spheroidal shape skew the equation. On one recent summer the North Pole enjoyed full-time light for over 190 days, rather than the expected 182.5 days. For an illuminating printout of sunrise and sunset for each day of the year in your hometown, send $15 to the U.S. Naval Observatory at 3450 Massachusetts Avenue NW, Washington D.C. 20392-5420.

Taking a Bearing

To take a bearing, point the directional arrow of your compass to the object whose bearing you want to know. Now rotate the compass dial so that the needle and the "N" indicator are aligned. Next, adjust for declination. The "N" indicator is now pointing to true north; the needle, as always, continues to point to magnetic north; and the directional arrow tells you the bearing of your landmark. (If this is confusing, try it out wherever you are reading this book. Even if you are indoors — shoot a bearing from the couch to the television set, or bookshelf, or the kitchen door.)

mountains invariably reach highways, but they are usually built in networks that can be confusing or misleading. A descending fork may dead-end in a valley clear-cut. Generally, the wider the road, the better your chances that it leads out.

When following a watercourse, consider what part of the country you are in and the type of terrain within your immediate vicinity. In the East, streams may end in swamps, which should never be crossed, even if frozen; they tend to be fouled with foot-tangling brush and potholes. In the North Woods, rivers often meander; when they are covered with ice, you may not be able to correctly determine the direction of flow, and if you do, you may end up at a lake anyway. Creeks in the West most reliably discharge into larger rivers, which are more often than not paralleled by highways; at the same time, the creek may flow through daunting thicket or narrow canyon before it gets to the river.

Population density of the immediate region should be considered before following fences, railroad tracks, or powerlines. Especially in the West, these might go on for a long stretch of wilderness; if barbed wire encloses a 20,000-acre, roughly square cattle ranch, it will be almost 6 miles on each side.

You may try backtracking along the prints you left in the snow on your way in, but conditions may make it difficult or impossible to do so. Footprints can be erased by wind-driven snow drift, or they may be absent in the first place if you crossed a large expanse of bare ground or frozen lake.

If backtracking is impractical, you might under certain conditions attempt the "bicycle-spoke" method. You must be sure that you will leave prints and that they will not be covered over for at least an hour; you must also have a strong expectation of getting unlost by reaching a point no farther than a mile from your original position from which you can identify familiar or populated surroundings.

First, mark your starting point — the point at which you became lost — and mark it so it will stay marked. Use deadfall branches to make a tepee and pack snow around the bases so wind does not blow the branches over; build a high, hard-packed snow pillar; or tie a piece of clothing around a tree trunk.

Set off in a fixed direction, using a compass or a landmark. Proceed for 30 minutes, and return if you don't find the tracks you made before becoming lost, the trail, or a familiar landmark. Repeat in the second most likely direction and so on until you succeed in, or choose to give up on, locating a way out. Be rational and realistic, don't exceed your physical resources of the moment, and stick to your plan; that ridge up ahead may well give you a better vantage point, but it is also 2 miles distant and 500 feet high. Never deviate from a straight course; changing directions at the far end of your probe is a sure path to compounding the original problem.

STAYING PUT. If you have notified someone back home of the general location of your trek, your expected return time, and the time at which they should assume you have encountered trouble and need help (something you should always do) remaining in place is often the correct course. This is especially true if

you are equipped for a night outdoors, or if a party member has suffered an injury that is not critical but
mitigates against movement.

If you choose to wait for rescue,
you'll wish to take several steps that
are discussed in detail elsewhere.
Build a fire, for warmth as well as to
mark your location (see page 205);
erect a shelter; if available, distribute

THE NORTH POLE

Santa faces a navigational challenge when he wends his way
home after his annual mission.
That's because, for purposes of
route finding, there are actually
two North Poles.

The point that we generally
picture is called the *geographic*
pole. This is the top of the
"spindle" around which the Earth
revolves, located at precisely 90
degrees north latitude.

But when you consult your
compass, its needle points to the
magnetic North Pole. This point,
at which the magnetic attraction is
straight down, is the more inter-
esting of the two, because it won't
sit still.

Since 1831, when the mag-
netic pole was discovered by Sir
James Ross, it has moved over
440 miles. Scientists speculate
this is due to shifting of the
planet's molten core, or to the
gravitational influence of other
bodies in the solar system. To
complicate matters further, the
magnetic pole travels a circadian

ellipse whose longer axis ranges
from 30 to 50 miles.

Frustrated in pinpointing the
current location, we contacted
Bezal Jesudason, who leads expeditions by airplane to both the
geographic and magnetic poles out
of his base at Resolute Bay, Northwest Territories, Canada. We
asked, "How do you know when
you are at the magnetic pole?"

"If your car keys are in your
pocket," Bezal replied solemnly,
"your pants fall down."

You can get to the North Pole
fairly easily, if expensively, these
days. A number of adventure-
travel companies offer trips by
ice-breaker ocean liner or by airplane. Jesudason's organization,
High Arctic International, provides guided flights in March of
each year, at a cost of about
$8,000 per person.

What you'll usually find at the
pole is ice covering water 13,410
feet deep. But sometimes, even in
the height of winter, strong cur-
rents will open leads of exposed
water at the pole itself.

food; and treat or prevent any medical conditions.

But your major duty, as far as helping your rescuers, is to make it as easy as possible for them to find you, and to aid them in pinpointing your position when they do. Depending on your location and the resources of your area search-and-rescue personnel, help may arrive overland or by helicopter. Make preparations for either.

Since your party may be obscured from above because it is within shelter, under trees, or there is some other obstruction, build visual signals in an open area near your temporary camp. A large fire is ideal, especially at night, but if your party is especially tired it may not be able to fuel it. Otherwise, and if there is sufficient deadfall wood, assign fire-tending duties in 1-hour shifts.

Tromp out a message in the snow in broad block letters at least 10 feet high. While "SOS" is traditional, it isn't necessary; any pattern that is clearly not naturally created, such as an X, will serve. To make it stand out against the white background, cover it with conifer boughs, rocks, or anything you are carrying that you don't need for warmth: backpacks, skis, poles, snowshoes, and spare clothing. Be sure to weigh down lighter items against wind gusts and periodically sweep it clear if snow is falling.

Be prepared to guide in a rescue party when you hear it approach or perhaps sight it at some distance below you. If rescuers are coming in without motorized vehicles, a marine- or police-quality whistle makes a piercing noise that can be heard at some distance. Get out in the open and as high up as is practical, and stay away from the obscuring noise of running water.

HIGH-TECH HELP

Several electronic devices address getting lost. The high-band radio transceiver has been around for decades, and in some backcountry areas you can even use a cellular phone. But many enthusiasts consider these antithetical to the wilderness experience; we head into the wilderness to get away, not to stay in touch.

The global positioning system is more tolerated, partly because it puts you in contact not with a person but with the $12 billion, 24-satellite NAVSTAR system, but mostly because it is so darn neat.

The GPS was developed by the Pentagon to guide missiles to their targets. You can take advantage of it with the help of a gizmo that determines where it is by analyzing input from three or more of

continued on next page

the satellites in the NAVSTAR system.

The GPS unit, about the size of a TV remote control and vaguely similar in appearance, is a rudimentary computer with display and keyboard. Features of various models include a steering mode that tells you how close you are to your target and when to turn in either direction; display of your compass bearing, speed, and time of arrival; and, of course, your location, as denoted by longitude and latitude (you'll want to use it in conjunction with a map). Interestingly, the locating feature is not as accurate as it could be; the Department of Defense slightly distorts the signal that civilian GPS units can receive, to make them less effective to our enemies, real and perceived. Still, it will indicate where you are to within about 50 feet.

When used conscientiously, a GPS device makes it impossible to become lost. The "go to" function allows you to check your position periodically and store it in memory. If you must retrace your way, the display guides you back along your stored path, even showing the correct compass heading.

GPS devices suitable for winter activities are priced from $300 to $1,000. Costlier models offer larger displays and more optional features; at least one can interface with a personal computer.

If you are approached from the air, illumination is your ally. At night, a fire remains the best bet, but waving a flashlight — or several flashlights — may be effective if the chopper is low enough and the searchers vigilant. On a sunny day, reflect the rays with a mirror, metal utensil, or a piece of aluminum foil.

There are various signal codes for indicating subtleties of your situation, but because you'll rarely have occasion to use them we recommend that you concentrate on the single most important: Three of anything — flashlight blinks, fires, whistle blasts, or even party members waving their hands in the air — indicates "Send Help."

AVALANCHES

I was sixteen years old the first time I went backcountry skiing in high country, and had read just enough about avalanches to know they existed and to understand some rudimentary idea about their behavior.

Presently I found myself in the Colorado Rockies, at the top of a steep, narrow gulley that was heavily laden with snow.

"Hey, is this the kind of slope that avalanches?" I said to my companion. For emphasis, I stamped a ski the way I'd seen avalanche patrollers do in the movies to test loose cornices.

Suddenly the slope below us broke away and disappeared with a rush of snow into the gulley. Yes, indeed, it was an avalanche slope.

Only through the watchfulness that fate affords to dumb kids did we happen to be above it; otherwise we would have been buried in the bottom of the gulley under several feet of snow.

Now that I am older and live in the mountains, I have made it my business to learn a lot more about avalanche behavior and to give the phenomenon the respect it commands. Perhaps the most frightening aspect is that, as with earthquakes, even the world's most knowledgeable

---

FIRING UP

If you do need to build a signal fire, under most conditions the problem won't be wet wood. New snow is a surprisingly dry substance until melted and imparts almost no moisture to what it covers.

However, it is nearly impossible to ignite a log, let alone a twig, with a match or a Bic lighter. You'll need tinder for a firestarter. The best is commercial fire paste or fire strips, volatile but nonflaring materials that flame up easily.

If neither is in your kit, you may be able to find a substitute lying beneath the snow all around you, courtesy of Mother Nature. Trees wish to remain moist and

free of disease and fungal infection, and the substances that provide this protection are in their fallen leaves and needles. Scientists call them aromatics, waxes, oils, aliphatics, and polyphenols; we call them stuff that burns good.

Graeme Berlyn of the Yale School of Forestry and Environmental Studies suggests that in the Pacific region, you look for chaparral, which can burn like pure oil. The fallen dried needles of conifers found across the continent — from Douglas fir in the Rockies to yellow pine in the Southeast — are so fuel intense that they will occasionally produce a blue flame. Back east, says Berlyn, search out the leaves of rhododendron, azalea, and mountain laurel.

authorities can't tell you exactly if or when a slope will avalanche.

The only prudent approach is to avoid slopes on which conditions make a slide possible. For a backcountry trekker, this sometimes means forgoing the most attractive mountainsides of deep powder.

The mechanics of avalanches comprise a complex science involving snow structure, slope steepness, changing weather patterns, and a myriad of other factors (see Chapter 6 on snow and ice to learn about some of the types of snow that are prone to avalanche). Here we'll emphasize the basic circumstances under which they occur, the rules for avoiding being present for the event, and what

The Ortovox F1 Focus avalanche transceiver operates at a more powerful frequency than previous models providing a greater range.

TRANSCEIVERS AND HOW TO USE THEM

An avalanche transceiver is a small radio transmitter and receiver worn under clothing. While transceivers no doubt have helped in many rescues, they should not in any way be regarded as a foolproof shield against injury or death by avalanche. Backcountry veterans have a saying about transceivers: "They're handy for showing you where to find the corpse."

Transceivers have two modes, send and receive. When a party sets out into the backcountry, all members set their transceivers on "send," which means they emit a beeping radio signal. If one or several members of the party are buried by an avalanche, the others switch their sets to "receive" and comb the avalanche debris in a grid pattern. When they approach the victim, they'll pick up the beeping of his transceiver in their earplug. The nearer they are, the louder the beeping.

More specific instructions for conducting the search can be found in the instruction manuals for transceivers, and you should practice with them before the actual event of an avalanche.

to do if you or one of your party are caught.

When and Where Avalanches Tend to Occur

Most avalanches slide during or immediately after storms. At this stage, the snow hasn't yet settled and is more prone to movement, and slopes tend to be most unstable. Be especially cautious when the fall is heavy, accumulating at a rate of more than 1 inch per hour. This condition tends to load the slope with unstabilized weight. Depending on wind and temperature, snow requires 2 or 3 days to "set up" after a storm, and even then it's not at all certain that other conditions won't cause it to avalanche.

Avalanches are most likely on slopes between 30 and 45 degrees;

An avalanche in progress. While you can learn how to recognize avalanche-prone terrain and snow conditions, no one can accurately predict when one will occur.

steeper than that and the snow tends to slide off in harmless "sluffs." A hand-held device called an inclinometer will accurately measure a slope's declivity.

Avalanches favor areas where the wind has deposited deep snow on a lee slope. Watch for cornices (over-hangs of windpacked snow), which can break off, and the areas immediately below cornices, which will probably be laden with wind-driven snow. Avalanche "starting zones" often occur at the tops of gullies, bowls, and lee-facing ridges; look for these formations and avoid crossing them.

Although avalanches are associated in the popular mind with the high mountains of the West, which in fact is where they are most common, you enjoy no special security in other regions. We've triggered the breakoff of a large cornice on a windswept knob in the Upper Peninsula of Michigan.

Avoiding Avalanches

Choosing a safe route is the easiest and surest way to avoid avalanches, short of staying out of the mountains altogether. Traverse the middle of the valley floor far from steep slopes — although, like earthfalls, avalanches have been known to run a quarter mile across valleys and up opposite slopes. If you are ascending a mountain, stick to the ridgetops and densely forested areas. Dense stands of trees serve to anchor the snow in place; avalanches tend to occur on open or lightly forested slopes. Avoid steep, open slopes. Note past avalanche paths: Look for a slope devoid of trees or one with trees that are shorn of branches on one side.

Study the slopes around you for recent avalanche activity. If you see fresh avalanche debris, note the steepness and aspect of the slope on which it occurs, and give the slope a pass. If you must cross a potential avalanche path, do so either with a belay or one person at a time, with other party members keeping a close eye on the person crossing.

Learn the snow conditions that are more prone to avalanche than others. A good guide is *ABC of Avalanche Safety* (see Sources & Resources). The snow conditions found in spring often make this the best time to ski or travel in the backcountry. In spring, the loose or unconsolidated layers of the snowpack that could slip loose in an avalanche begin to meld into a solid mass. The sun warms the snow to the melting point during the middle of the day and the night cold refreezes the snow particles together, like cement. If you travel in the early morning, when the snow is still frozen in a mass, the avalanche danger is minimized. Later in the day, however, the sun's warmth thaws and loosens the snow and you should avoid steep slopes.

What to Do If Caught in an Avalanche

As with most backcountry hazards, the best way to avoid an avalanche is to stay out of a potential path in the first place. But this is no guarantee you won't confront one, and you should be prepared for that eventuality. Ideally, each member of the party should carry an avalanche transceiver (see "Transceivers and How to Use Them," page 206), ski poles that fit together to form an avalanche probe, and a lightweight shovel.

EMERGENCY AND SURVIVAL GEAR

We are forgetful, and so we make lists. The one that follows is a detailed catalog of devices, personal items, repair ingredients, and general tchotchkes (a handy Yiddish word roughly translated as "doo-dads") that are relevant to comfort, emergencies, and survival. Bear in mind that there are few anticipated circumstances in which you would carry them all; if you did, your pack would be the size of a car trunk. Heed the pointers given throughout this book, along with your bank of experience, to decide which are necessary or desirable for any given activity.

One efficient way to use this list is to input it into a computer file. When preparing for a trek, copy it to a temporary file and go through it, deleting whatever is inappropriate given expected conditions.

FIRST-AID KIT

Whistle	Camp shovel	GPS unit
Flashlight	Sunglasses	Swiss Army knife or
Disposable plastic	Goggles	Leatherman tool
lighter/waterproof	Sunscreen Aluminum	Avalanche transceiver
matches	foil	Avalanche probe
Fire paste	Duct tape	Collapsible shovel
Chapstick	Pencil and paper	Wristwatch
Vaseline	Map	Water bottle
Axe/saw	Compass	Coins for pay phone

If you are caught in an avalanche, try to discard your skis, poles, snow-shoes, or any other equipment that can encumber you, and make swim-ming motions with your arms and legs to help keep yourself on the surface. Victims who have survived report feeling the avalanche slowing, and at

Cornices like this one, where drifting causes snow to pile up on the lee side of ridges, are especially susceptible to avalanches. Go up and around such cornices to avoid triggering a snow slide.

this point managed to poke a hand above the snow as they came to a rest, "flagging" their location to other members of their party. Cup the other hand or arm near your face to create a breathing pocket in the snow.

If you are a member of a party in which someone is caught in an avalanche, it is imperative to keep an eye on the victim, or the victim's last visible location, and begin your search in a swath downhill of that site. You must dig the victim out before suffocation. After 10 minutes of burial in the snow, the chances of surviving drop off dramatically, but you shouldn't give up the search. In extraordinary cases, victims have survived for over 24 hours.

S O U R C E S &
R E S O U R C E S

OK, you've read the book (or perhaps you've dipped into several chapters). Now you want to know where to find more information. Following are places to contact, more books to read, and ideas about acquiring equipment.

ORGANIZATIONS & ASSOCIATIONS

If you are looking for company, for clubs, or simply for information, call any of these organizations. They are all eager to promote their sport. Often they will have lists of local groups or individuals that you can contact. There are so many such organizations, in fact, that we cannot possibly list them all or give information that will stay current. However, we can get you started. These leading educational organizations, listed by sport in the order that they appear in *Winter Adventure*, are considered the best in the field:

SLEDDING

U.S. BOBSLED AND SKELETON FEDERATION
P. O. Box 828
Lake Placid, NY 12946
518-523-1842
Fax: 518-523-9491
Conducts youth and development programs to prepare athletes for Olympic and U.S. competitions. Call to locate local clubs and outfitters.

U.S. LUGE ASSOCIATION
P.O. Box 651
35 Church Street
Lake Placid, NY 12946
518-523-2071
Fax: 518-523-4106
Governing body of the sport of luge in the United States.

(NATURBAHN) MARQUETTE LUGE ASSOCIATION
P. O. Box 931
Marquette, MI 49855
906-475-5843
Call for more information on naturbahn. The association

oversees the only certified naturban track in the U.S. and reports plans for new tracks at Lake Placid, New York; Mount Hood, Oregon; and Duluth, Minnesota.

SNOWSHOEING

U.S. SNOWSHOE ASSOCIATION
RD Box 94, Route 25
Corinth, NY 12822
518-654-7648
Promotes snowshoeing for recreation and serves as the national governing body for amateur snowshoe racing.

DOG SLEDDING, SKIJORING

INTERNATIONAL FEDERATION OF SLED DOG SPORTS
7118 North Beehive Road
Pocatello, ID 83201
208-232-5130
Fax: 208-234-1608
National and international sled-dog racing groups represented.

INTERNATIONAL SLED DOG RACING ASSOCIATION
P.O. Box 446
Nordman, ID 83848
208-443-3153
Fax: 208-443-3052
Sanctions major races.

LAKES REGION SLED DOG CLUB
P. O. Box 382
Laconia, NH 03247
603-279-5063
Promotes sled dog racing, especially in New England and Canada.

SNOWBOARDING
INTERNATIONAL SNOWBOARD FEDERATION
P.O. Box 477
Vale, CO 81658
303-949-5473

SKI INDUSTRIES AMERICA
8377B-Greensboro Drive
MacLean, VA 22102
703-556-9020
Fax: 703-821-8276
Non-profit trade association of ski, on-snow, and outdoor action sports equipment.

U.S. AMATEUR SNOWBOARD ASSOCIATION
P.O. Box 4869
Breckinridge, CO 80424
303-453-7928

ICE SKATING, HOCKEY, BROOMBALL
AMATEUR SPEEDSKATING UNION OF THE UNITED STATES
1033 Shady Lane
Glen Ellyn, IL 60137
708-790-3230/ 800-634-4766
Fax: 708-790-3235
Conducts local training programs and national speedskating competitions. Also maintains the Speedskating Hall of Fame.

CANADIAN BROOMBALL FEDERATION
Percy Page Centre
11759 Groat Road
Edmonton, AB
Canada T5M 3K6
403-453-8527
Fax: 403-460-0527

FEDERATION OF BROOMBALL ASSOCIATIONS OF ONTARIO
1220 Sheppard Avenue
East Willowdale, ONT
Canada M2K 2X1
This organization publishes a newsletter 3 times per year.

U.S.A. HOCKEY
4965 North 30th Street
Colorado Springs, CO 80919
719-599-5500
Fax: 719-599-5994
This is the governing body for amateur ice hockey in the U.S. Organizes leagues, arranges tournaments and sponsors clinics for coaches and referees.

U.S. FIGURE SKATING ASSOCIATION
20 First Street
Colorado Springs, CO 80906
719-635-5200
Fax: 719-635-9548
National governing body for amateur ice figure skating in the U.S.

U.S. INTERNATIONAL SPEEDSKATING ASSOCIATION
P.O. Box 16157
Rocky River, OH 44116
216-899-0128
Fax: 216-899-0109
Promotes U.S. speedskaters in Olympic and international competition. Also conducts summer camps.

ICEBOATING, SKATE SAILING, ICE SURFING
INTERNATIONAL DN ICE YACHT RACING ASSOCIATION
3497 East Erie Avenue
Lorain, OH 44052
216-288-2510
Promotes ice yacht racing.

SKATE SAILING ASSOCIATION OF AMERICA
1252 Crim Road
Bridgewater, NJ 08807
908-722-9490
Promotes the sport of skate sailing and conducts races.

WORLD ICE/SNOW ASSOCIATION
P. O. Box 414
Jamestown, RI 02835
401-423-1511
Fax: 401-423-0490
Promotes the young sport of ice surfing.

CURLING/BARRELS
U.S. BARREL JUMPING ASSOCIATION
950 Wolverine Drive
Walled Lake, MI 48390
810-624-0066/810-669-1171
Compiles statistics and sponsors annual barrel jumping competitions, on both ice and roller skates.

U.S. CURLING ASSOCIATION
1100 Center Point Drive
P. O. Box 866
Stevens Point, WI 54481
715-344-1199
Fax: 715-344-6885
A federation of regional curling associations and their member clubs, which sponsors national curling championships and is also active in international competitions.

CANADIAN CURLING ASSOCIATION
1600 James Naismith Drive
Gloucester, ONT
Canada K1B 5N4
613-748-5628/613-748-5713

U.S. WOMEN'S CURLING ASSOCIATION
4114 North 53rd Street
Omaha, NE 68104
402-453-6574
This group is affiliated with the USCA.

WORLD CURLING FEDERATION
81 Great King Street
Edinburgh EH3 6RN
Scotland
44315564884
Fax: 44315569400
Works to establish rules for curling in international competition and operates world curling competitions.

WINTER CAMPING
ADIRONDACK
MOUNTAIN CLUB
RR 3 P. O. Box 3055
Lake George, NY 12845-9523
518-668-4447/518-668-3746
Conducts various recreational, conservation, and educational activities. Annually sponsors winter mountaineering schools and environmental workshops.

APPALACHIAN
MOUNTAIN CLUB
5 Joy Street
Boston, MA 02108
617-523-0636
Fax 617-523-0722
Almost 55,000 members; the Club offers numerous hiking programs from 2-5 days.

COLORADO MOUNTAIN CLUB
2530 West Alameda Avenue
Denver, CO 80219
303-922-8976

MOUNTAINEERS
300 3rd Avenue West
Seattle, WA 98119
206-284-6310/206-284-4977
Conducts short hiking, skiing, camping, and mountain climbing trips for members, in the northwest region.

PACIFIC CREST TRAIL
ASSOCIATION
5325 Elkhorn Boulevard,
Suite 256
Sacramento, CA 95842
800-817-2243

TOUR OPERATORS, OUTFITTERS, & SCHOOLS
The organizations and guides below offer a variety of programs, or can recommend other sources to you. For more listings, check out the back pages of the magazines following.

MOUNTAINEERING, WINTER CAMPING, ICE CLIMBING
AMERICAN ALPINE INSTITUTE
1212 24th
Bellingham, WA 98225
206-671-1505
International courses in mountaineering, ice-climbing and winter skills and rescue.

AMERICAN MOUNTAIN
GUIDES ASSOCIATION
710 10th Street, Suite 101
Golden, CO 80401
303-271-0984
Call for a nationwide referral list of mountain-guide services.

ALPINE SKILLS
INTERNATIONAL
P. O. Box 8
Norden, CA 95724
916-426-9108
Ski mountaineering, ice-climbing, winter skills.

BACKROADS
1516 5th Street, Suite A200
Berkeley, CA 94710-1740
800-462-2848
Fax: 510-527-1444
Considered the foremost active travel company.

BOULDER OUTDOOR
SURVIVAL SCHOOL
P. O. Box 3226
Flagstaff, AZ 86003
801-335-7404 (summer)
208-356-7446 (winter)
Winter shelters, making snowshoes, dogsledding, winter first aid.

CANADA NORTH OUTFITTING
P. O. Box 3100
87 Mill Street
Almonte, ONT
Canada K0A 1A0
613-256-4057
Tours in the Canadian Arctic and subarctic.

CANADIAN OUTWARD BOUND
WILDERNESS SCHOOL
P. O. Box 116, Station S
Toronto, ONT
Canada M5M 4L6
416-787-1721
Winter courses geared for youth, include dogsledding, skiing, and snow-camping.

COLORADO
MOUNTAIN SCHOOL
P. O. Box 2062
Estes Park, CO 80517
800-444-0730/303-567-5758
Mountaineering, ice-climbing.

ECOTOURISM SOCIETY
P.O. Box 755
North Bennington, VT 052757
802-447-2121
Keeps an eye on the environmental viability of programs others sponsor.

ELDERHOSTEL
75 Federal Street
Boston, MA 02210-1941
617-426-7788
Fax: 617-426-8351
Elderhostel's programs for older persons include a variety of outdoor sports and activities.

EXUM MOUNTAIN GUIDES
Grand Teton National Park
P. O. Box 56
Moose, WY 83012
307-733-2297
Full range of winter programs, from ice-climbing to ski touring.

**FANTASY RIDGE
GUIDE SERVICE**
c/o Michael Covington
P. O. Box 1679
Telluride, CO 81435
303-728-3546
*Ice-climbing in Colorado and
more exotic alpine expeditions.*

**INTERNATIONAL
ALPINE SCHOOL**
Boulder Mountain Guides
P. O. Box 3037
Eldorado Springs, CO 80025
303-494-4904
*Snow and glacier skills
training; ice-climbing.*

**INTERNATIONAL MOUNTAIN
CLIMBING SCHOOL**
Dept 3, P. O. Box 1666
North Conway, NH 03860
603-356-7064
Short courses in climbing.

**JACKSON HOLE MOUNTAIN
GUIDES & CLIMBING SCHOOL**
P. O. Box 7477
165 N. Glenwood
Jackson, WY 83001
307-733-4979
*Full range of winter climbing
and mountaineering.*

MOUNTAIN GUIDES ALLIANCE
P. O. Box 266
North Conway, NH 03860
603-356-5310
*Ice-climbing programs, custom-
arranged.*

**NATIONAL OUTDOOR
LEADERSHIP SCHOOL (NOLS)**
288 Main Street
P. O. Box AA
Lander, WY 82520
307-332-6973
*Winter sports programs include
Telemarking, avalanche safety,
and winter shelter construction.*

OUTWARD BOUND
Rt. 9-D
R 2, Box 280
Garrison, NY 10524
800-243-8520
*Conducts winter outdoor pro-
grams in a number of states.*

RAINIER MOUNTAINEERING
535 Dock Street
Tacoma, WA 98402
206-627-6242
*Snow and ice-climbing on Mt.
Rainier, glacier camping.*

SPECIAL ODYSSEYS
3430 Evergreen Point Road
P. O. Box 37A
Medina, WA 98039
206-455-1960
*Offers multi-activity trips on ice
and in the wilderness.*

**DOGSLEDDING
OUTFITTERS,
TOUR GUIDES**
**BOMHOFF'S ALASKAN
SLED DOG KENNEL**
HC-89, P. O. Box 256
Willow, AK 99688
907-495-6470
Fax: 907-495-6471
*Sled dog tours including 4- to
9-day trips.*

**BOUNDARY
COUNTRY TREKKING**
Gunflint Trail HC64
P. O. Box 590
Grand Marais, MN 55604
800-322-8327
Sled dog outfitter.

**CARIBOU CREEK
SLED DOG SCHOOL**
P. O. Box 196
Shatham, MI 49816
906-439-5747
*Three- to 8-day wilderness
treks, racing school for mushers.*

**CHUGACH EXPRESS
DOG SLED TOURS**
P. O. Box 261
Girdwood, AK 99587
907-783-2266
Sled dog outfitter.

MAHOOSUC GUIDE SERVICE
Bear River Road
Newry, ME 04261
207-824-2073
*Dogsledding instruction, 1- to
7-day trips in Maine and
eastern Arctic.*

SOURDOUGH OUTFITTERS
P. O. Box 90
Bettles, AK 99726
907-692-5252
Fax: 907-692-5612
Sled dog outfitter.

SUSITINA DOG TOURS
HC 89, Box 464
Willow, AK 99688
907-495-6324
*One- to 5-day trips from lodge
near Denali (Mount McKinley).*

**WINTERGREEN
DOGSLEDDING LODGE**
(featured in Trailside® video)
Ring Rock Road
Ely, MN 55731
800-584-9425/218-365-6022
*Three- to 4-day lodge-to-lodge
treks, 5-to 8-night camping trips.*

**FIRST AID AND
SAFETY COURSES**
**AMERICAN AVALANCHE
INSTITUTE**
P. O. Box 308
Wilson, WY 83014
307-733-3315
Avalanche safety.

**AMERICAN RED CROSS
NATIONAL HEADQUARTERS**
431 18th Street N.W.
Washington, D.C. 20006
202-737-8300
*For first aid and CPR classes
call the American Red Cross
and ask for chapter information.*

**STONEHEARTH OPEN
LEARNING OPPORTUNITIES,
INC. (SOLO)**
P. O. Box 3150
Conway, NH 03818
603-447-6711
*Wilderness and emergency med-
ical courses.*

**WILDERNESS
MEDICAL ASSOCIATES**
RFD 2 Box 890
Bryant Pond, ME 04219
800-742-2931
*Training specialists in emer-
gency medicine and wilderness
rescue.*

MAGAZINES

Magazines these days can be so filled with photographs and stirring narratives that they are almost as satisfying as being there yourself. So use these for inspiration and information, but don't stop there.

DOGSLEDDING

HUSKY FEVER

Northern News Services
P. O. Box 2212
Yellowknife, N.W. T.
Canada X0E 1H0

MUSHING

P.O. Box 149
Ester, AK 99725
907-479-0454
This magazine can be read on the www at http://www.polarnet.fnsb.ak.us/u sers/mushing Information on the growing sports of dogsledding, skijoring, carting, dog-packing, and weight-pulling.

TEAM & TRAIL

P.O. Box 128
Center Harbor, NH 03226
603-253-6265
Worldwide news on dogsled races.

ICE SKATING

SKATING

U.S. Figure Skating
Association
20 First Street
Colorado Springs, CO 80906
719-635-5200
The journal of the national organization for this sport.

ICE HOCKEY

HOCKEY MAGAZINE

The Publishing Group, Inc.
1022 W. 80th Street
Bloomington, MN 55420
612-881-3183
Covers all levels of hockey and related topics, including history.

HOCKEY PLAYER MAGAZINE

P. O. Box 7494
Northridge, CA 91327-7494
818-878-9573
Ice hockey and street hockey.

CURLING

UNITED STATES CURLING NEWS

1100 Center Point Drive
P. O. Box 866
Stevens Point, WI 54481
715-344-1199
News of curling associations and clubs, championships, and international competitions.

WINTER CAMPING, ICE CLIMBING, & BACKPACKING

BACKPACKER

Rodale Press, Inc.
P. O. Box 7590
Red Oak, IA 51591-0590
800-666-3434
Backpacker's annual guide to equipment is a must.

CLIMBING

1101 Village Road
Suite LL-1-B
Carbondale, CO 81623
970-963-9449
The premier climbing mag takes you all over the world; good listings of suppliers and manufacturers.

OUTSIDE MAGAZINE

Mariah Media Inc.
400 Market Street
Santa Fe, NM 87501
(505) 989-7100/800-937-9710
All active outdoor sports, practically invented adventure travel.

ROCK & ICE

Eldorado Publishing Inc.
603A S. Broadway
Boulder, CO 80303-5926
303-499-8410
"America's #1 climbing magazine" makes an effort to cover all aspects of the sport.

SUMMIT

1221 May Street
Hood River, OR 97031
503-387-2200
A glossy mountaineering magazine with great photography and 40 years of experience.

SNOWBOARDING

SNOWBOARDER

P. O. Box 1028
Dana Point, CA 92629
714-496-5922
Just what the name says....

TRANSWORLD SNOWBOARDING

353 Airport Road
Oceanside, CA 92054
800-334-8152
One more...and....

WARP

353 Airport Road
Oceanside, CA 92054
800-334-8152
Surfing, skateboarding, snowboarding (+ music!).

WINTER SURFING ON THE INTERNET

Alas, any section such as this one is out of date within a few days. If you're experienced on the Internet you will have no trouble locating the subjects that interest you. But, just for fun, here are some we found:

Mushing magazine has a worldwide web site with a long list of dogsled organizations and tours you can join. Here's where it's at: *http://www.polarnet.fnsb.ak. us/us ers/mushing*

There's a wonderful Climber Directory of actual climbers in both the US and Canada; if you're curious, try: *http://www.dtek.chalmers.se/Cli mbing/Directory/index* and the Climbing Dictionary is just what it says : *http://www.fm.bs.dlr.de/dlr/abt_*

12/climbing/climbing_dict.html
Climbing Archive! contains a climbing FAQ ("frequently asked questions") and tips on where to go climbing in gyms and the outdoors in Canada, Europe, Asia, the United States, and Australia.
http://www.gnn.com/gnn/wic/sports.22.html

There are probably lots of newsgroups; check out *rec.sport.skating.ice.recreation* or *rec.skiing.snowboard.*

If you are intrigued by the mystery of snow and ice, check the www page of the National Snow and Data Center *http://nsidc.colorado.edu*

TRAILSIDE®: MAKE YOUR OWN ADVENTURE
Trailside's service can be accessed via keyword "Trailside" (the address is *http://io.datasys.swri.edu/TSide.html*). The Trailside service provides information from the television series' program guides as well as a bulletin board, Campfire Chats, Trailside Outfitter, Maps and Snaps, and complete gear lists from ongoing Trailside adventures.

BOOKS
Sure, you're going to put on those skates and brave the cold. But first, another book to satisfy your need to read all about it first.

SNOWSHOEING
Snowshoe Book, Leslie Hurley and William Osgood. 1983. $10.95. Viking Penguin.

Snowshoeing, Sally Edwards and Melissa McKenzie. 1995. $13.95. Human Kinetics.

Snowshoeing, Gene Prater. 3rd ed. 1988. $10.95. The Mountaineers.
Everything you ever wanted to

know about snowshoeing. The author's personal experiences snowshoeing all over North America add authority to his accounts of regional variations in the sport.

DOG SLEDDING AND SKIJORING
Joy of Running Sled Dogs,: a Step-By-Step Guide to Training and Enjoying Sled Dogs, Noel K. Flanders. 1988. $9.95. Alpine Publications.
This manual for the beginner is particularly strong on choosing and training dogs.

Skijor With Your Dog, Carol Kaynor and Mari Hoe-Raitto. 1992. $14.95. OK Publishing.
Covers the techniques of the sport, and also trail etiquette, winter camping, racing, and skijoring for children and the disabled. Includes a chapter on Nordic-style mushing with a *pulk.*

SNOWBOARDING
Complete Book of Snowboarding, K.C. Althen. 1990.$17.95. Charles E. Tuttle.
A step-by-step, easy-to-use guide for the beginner snowboarder. Includes information about equipment and ski areas.

Complete Snowboarder, Jeff Bennett and Scott Downey. 1994. $14.95. Ragged Mountain Press.

Freestyle Skiing and Snowboarding, Robert Guthrie. 1992. $12.95. Capstone Press. A young adult/children's guide to the sport.

Snowboarding Know-How, Christof Weiss. 1993. $10.95. Sterling Publishing, Inc.
A young adult introductory guide to the sport.

NATURE OF SNOW AND ICE
Secret Language of Snow, Terry Tempest Williams and Ted Major. 1984. $10.95. Sierra Club/Pantheon Books.
Aimed at young adults, this book also contains information valuable to a general audience on types of snow and the natural world of winter.

OBSERVING THE NATURAL WORLD
Animal Tracks, Chris Stall. $5.95 each. Mountaineers Books.
A series of handy, pocket-sized field guides with tracks and information of the most common animals and birds in each region.

Exploring Nature in Winter, Alan M. Cvancara. 1992. $17.95. Walker and Company. The best recent book on the subject, this volume covers weather, botany, animal tracking, birding, astronomy, and photography.

Field Guide to Animal Tracks, Olaus J. Murie. 2nd ed. 1975. $15.95. The Peterson Field Guides Series. Houghton Mifflin. The volume to pack on winter safaris, with illustrations of the prints of nearly 100 critters.

Field Guide to Tracking Animals in Snow, Louise R. Forrest. 1988. $14.95. Stackpole Books.

Life in the Cold: an Introduction to Winter Ecology, Peter Marchand. 2nd ed. 1991. $16.95. University Press of New England.
A fine introduction to winter ecology which includes chapters on how plants and animals survive in winter under the snow and ice, how the snowpack changes, and how the human body responds to cold temperatures.

Tracking and the Art of Seeing: How to Read Animal Tracks and Signs, Paul Rezendes. 1992. $19.95. Firefly Books, Ltd.

ICE SKATING; HOCKEY

Sports Illustrated Hockey, Jack Falla. 1987. $9.95. Sports Illustrated Books.
A guide for the entry-level hockey player. Includes a section on how to build a backyard rink.

Sports Illustrated Figure Skating, John M. Petkevich. 1989. $10.95. Sports Illustrated Books.
An illustrated guide that covers everything from the snowplow stop to the reverse double lute.

ICE CLIMBING

Climbing Ice, Yvon Chouinard. 1978. $20.00. Sierra Club Books.

Climbing in the Adirondacks: a Guide to Rock and Ice Routes, Don Mellor. 2nd ed. 1993. $24.95. Adirondack Mountain Club.

Ice World : Techniques and Experiences of Modern Ice Climbing, Jeff Lowe. 1996. Mountaineers Books.

Mountaineering : the Freedom of the Hills , Don Graydon, ed. 5th ed. 1992. Mountaineers. Defines climbing techniques, snow and glacier travel and much more.

CURLING

Curling Handbook, Roy Thiessen. $5.95. Hancock House Publishers, Ltd.

WINTER CAMPING

Active Travel Resource Guide, Daniel Browdy, ed. 1995. $19.95. Ultimate Ventures. Offers detailed information on over 3300 trips worldwide, from animal trekking and hiking to snow sports.

AMC Guide to Winter Camping, Stephen Gorman. 1991. $12.95. Appalachian Mountain Club Books.
In addition to treating gear and technique, this guide includes sections on such less-often-addressed topics as group dynamics and leadership, and camping with children.

Ski Camping: a Guide to the Delights of Back-Country Skiing, Ron Watters. 1989. $14.95. Great Rift Press. Clothing, overland travel tips, camping and cooking, route finding, hazards and emergencies.

Snow Caves for Fun and Survival, Ernest Wilkinson. 1992. $9.95. Johnson Books. How to construct snow caves, igloos, quinzhees, trenches, and other snow shelters, along with tips on clothing and winter camping.

Wilderness Skiing and Winter Camping, Chris Townsend. 1993. $17.95. Ragged Mountain Press.
The last word in winter camping. Townsend brings an international perspective to the sport, which is helpful in understanding some of the equipment and techniques favored by Europeans. A comprehensive gear list in the appendix is particularly useful.

Winterwise: a Backpacker's Guide, John M. Dunn. 1995. The Adirondack Mountain Club. A compendium of tips on topics including layering, shelter, route-finding, and safety.

SAFETY IN THE WINTER OUTDOORS

ABC of Avalanche Safety, Edward R. LaChapelle. 2nd ed. 1985. $6.95. Mountaineers Books.
A concise, pocket-sized guide to introduce the backcountry

user to the basics of avalanche safety.

Avalanche Handbook, David McClung and Peter Schaerer. 2nd ed. 1993. $19.95. Mountaineers Books.

Cold Comfort: Keeping Warm in the Outdoors, Glenn Randall. 1987. $10.95. Lyons & Burford, Publishers.

Hypothermia, Frostbite and Other Cold Injuries: Prevention, Recognition and Prehospital Treatment, James A. Wilkerson, C.C. Bangs, and J.S. Hayward. 1986. $11.95. Mountaineers Books.

Medicine for Mountaineering and Other Wilderness Activities, James A. Wilkerson, ed. 4th ed. 1992. $16.95. Moutaineers Books.

Medicine for the Backcountry, Buck Tilton and Frank Hubbell. 2nd ed. 1994. $12.99. C. S. Books, Inc.

VIDEOS

Videos can be reassuring if you haven't got a club or local organization to help you get started.

Trailside®: Make Your Own Adventure
Our video series was originally broadcast on public television. All Trailside videos may be purchased by calling 800-872-4574. A catalog is available. The following episodes are relevant to our winter theme.
Backcountry Skiing in Colorado
Backcountry Skiing in Idaho
Climbing Mount Rainier
Dogsledding in Wisconsin
Ski Touring California's High Sierra
Wilderness 911
Winter Camping in Montana
Winter Camping in Yellowstone National Park

SNOWSHOEING

When the Snow is Too Deep to Walk. Shows how to decide on touring shoes vs. snowshoes, clothing, camping gear and food; includes information on avalanches, hypothermia and Telemarking.

DOG SLEDDING

Alaska's Great Race: the Susan Butcher Story. Recounts Susan Butcher's experiences in the Iditarod Trail Sled Dog Race.

Logan Challenge. Climbers take their husky dog teams up the slopes of Northern Canada's Mt. Logan.

Season of the Sled Dog. Presents the life of a sled dog musher in the Alaska backcountry and how she cares for and trains her dog team.

SNOWBOARDING

Boarding School. Instructions and demonstrations for beginner snowboarders and cross-over skiers of all ages.

Don't Pat the Dog. This video uses a unique visual teaching format that relies on a solid visual image, rather than lengthy verbal explanations.

Get Dialed In. Learn to Snowboard; the Complete Video Guide: contains step-by-step beginner and intermediate exercises and techniques.

Snow Shredders/Snow Thrills. Two videotapes featuring the top ranked ski and snowboard Hot Doggers slashing their way down the slopes.

SnoWhat? Captures the outrageous mischief and skill of two skier-snowboarders.

Transworld Snowboarding Magazine Presents Coming Down the Mountain: a mind-blowing 16mm film documenting the relentless progression of freestyle and extreme snowboarding.

Warren Miller's Steeper and Deeper. A 90 minute ski and snowboard adventure that literally spans the globe.

NATURE OF SNOW AND ICE

Snow. A ten minute program from the Primary Science Series, that explains how snowflakes are formed and how people live, work and play in the snow.

Winter Ice (2nd ed.). Explains the importance of ice in its many forms in nature.

OBSERVING THE NATURAL WORLD

Explore the Wilderness in Winter. Tracks and signs: demonstrates how to read tracks of animals that live in the American Great Plains during winter.

Tracking Wildlife. Offers tips on tracking and getting close to various North American animals in terrain as varied as the snowy wilderness of Wyoming to the muddy streams of your own backyard.

ICE SKATING/HOCKEY

Lightning on Ice. Alan Thicke hosts this program which explores the past, present and future of hockey. Includes rare footage from the Hockey Hall of Fame Museum.

How to Ice Skate. Champions Tai Babilonia and Randy Gardner guide you through the entire process of learning how to ice skate, from choosing a pair of skates to executing advanced moves on ice.

ICEBOATING

Flying on Ice. Townspeople in the Hudson Valley enjoy iceboating on weekends.

CURLING

Labatt Curling Instructional Series. Demonstrates the sport of curling with tips for beginners on the game and the necessary equipment.

Tip of the Iceman. Demonstrates curling techniques.

MAIL-ORDER SOURCES OF BOOKS & VIDEOS

ADVENTUROUS TRAVELER BOOKSTORE

P. O. Box 577
Hinesburg, VT 05461
800-282-3963/802-482-3330
Fax: 800-282-3963
E-mail: *books@atbook.com; on the World Wide Web — http://www.gorp.com/atbook.htm — search their full selection of 3,000 titles by keyword. Largest supplier of worldwide adventure travel books & maps.*

BACKCOUNTRY BOOKSTORE

P. O. Box 6235
Lynnwood, WA 90836-0235
206-290-7652
Books and videos on all outdoor activities, as well as knowledgeable staff.

VIDEO ACTION SPORTS, INC.

200 Suburban Road, Suite E
San Luis Obispo, CA 93401
800-727-6689; 805-543-4812
Fax: 805-541-8544
Catalog available.

L. L. BEAN

Casco Street
Freeport, ME 04032
800-727-6689
Retail store in Freeport, outlets and catalog sales. Books, videos, and audio tapes.

MAIL-ORDER SOURCES OF MAPS

MAP DISTRIBUTION
U.S. Geological Survey
P. O. Box 25286, Federal
Center
Denver, CO 80225
800-USA-MAPS
Publishes a list of current maps

OFFICE OF PUBLIC INQUIRIES
National Park Service
Room 1013
Washington, D.C. 20240
202-208-4747
Maps and folders for national parks, forests, seashores, and historical sites

U.S. FOREST SERVICE
Public Affairs Office
2nd Floor
Auditors Building
14th & Independence Avenue,
S.W.
Washington, D.C. 20250
202-205-1760
155 national forest maps

MAIL-ORDER SOURCES OF EQUIPMENT

For most of the activities described in this book you will find equipment at your local sporting goods store or outfitter. However, for the best quality, and for specialized equipment for such activities as winter camping, we recommend the excellent mail-order suppliers listed below. At the end of the section we've added some suppliers of very specific products mentioned in the text. For ice surfing supplies we recommend you try windsurfing shops in your region.

THE BOUNDARY WATERS CATALOG
(from Piragis
Northwoods Company)
105 North Central Avenue Ely,
MN 55731
800-223-6565

Piragis is the only easily-accessible source we know of for ski-joring equipment. The Boundary Waters Catalog is also strong on in-camp gear such as stoves, sleeping pads, chairs, and lightweight food.

CAMPMOR
P. O. Box 700-B
Saddle River, NJ 07458-0700
800-CAMPMOR
Although Campmor stocks everything from clothing to tents and sleeping bags, this company is also strong on climbing hardware such as crampons, ice axes, rope, and carabiners. Also has a "virtual store."

CLIMB HIGH
1861 Shelburne Road
Shelburne, VT 05482
802-985-5056
Specializes in rock- and ice-climbing gear; full line of ski mountaineering equipment and clothing.

IME (INTERNATIONAL MOUNTAIN EQUIPMENT)
Dept 3, P. O. Box 1666
North Conway, NH 03860
603-356-7064
Affiliated with International Mountain Climbing School (see page 214), offers full range of climbing and backpacking gear.

L.L. BEAN, INC.
Freeport, ME 04033-0001
800-221-4221
The dean of outfitters, Bean is best-known for quality clothing at reasonable prices, but check out the wooden kids' pull-sled and the classic toboggan.

MOUNTAIN TOOLS
140 Calle Del Oaks
Monterey, CA 93940-5711
408-393-1011
Specializes in rock- and ice-climbing gear; full line of ski mountaineering equipment and clothing.

PATAGONIA MAIL ORDER, INC.
1609 W. Babcock Street
P.O. Box 8900
Bozeman, MT 59715
800-638-6464
Patagonia was founded as a purveyor of climbing equipment by Yvon Chouinard, the noted mountaineer who redefined the ice axe. The company now concentrates on manufacturing clothing using such state-of-the-art materials as Capilene and Synchilla.

REI (RECREATIONAL EQUIPMENT, INC.)
1700 45th Street
Sumner, WA 98390
800-426-4840
Established in 1938, REI is one of the older catalog venders, offering a broad selection of quality name-brand clothing and camping equipment.

SIERRA TRADING POST
5025 Campstool Road
Cheyenne, WY 82007
307-775-8000
Principally a vender of clothing and footwear; Sierra also sells quality tents, backpacks, and sleeping bags, but selection of these items is not extensive.

And for those unusual, one-of-a kind products:

S&R MARINE
501 Hickory Street
Pewaukee, WI 53072
414-691-2230
For the "Nite" model iceboat.

SKYNASAUR CORP.
7070 W. 117th Avenue
Broomfield, CO 80020
303-466-4499
For kites for kite skiing.

PHOTO
CREDITS

INDEX